CW00943507

A Bush Calendar

A Bush Calendar

Amy. E. Mack

With illustrations by Robin Single

CORNSTALK PUBLISHING
an imprint of Angus & Robertson Publishers
Unit 4, Eden Park, 31 Waterloo Road,
North Ryde, NSW, Australia 2113;
94 Newton Road, Auckland 1,
New Zealand; and
16 Golden Square, London W1R 4BN,
United Kingdom

This book is copyright.
Apart from any fair dealing for the
purposes of private study, research,
criticism or review, as permitted
under the Copyright Act, no part may
be reproduced by any process without
written permission. Inquiries should
be addressed to the publishers.

First published in Australia
by Angus & Robertson Publishers in 1909
Reprinted 1924
Revised edition 1981
Reprinted 1982
This edition 1987
Reprinted in 1989

Copyright © Nancy Phelan and Sheila Smith-White 1909

National Library of Australia
Cataloguing-in-publication data

Mack, Amy Eleanor
  A bush calendar.

  Rev. ed.
  Previous ed.: Sydney:
  Angus & Robertson, 1909.
  ISBN 0 207 14278 5

  1. Natural history — New South Wales —
  Sydney. I. Title.

574.9944'1

Printed in Singapore

To
The one who showed me the way

Acacia suaveolens

AUGUST

ACCORDING to the official calendar it is still winter, but out in the bush all the world knows it is spring. Although the week's heavy rain has drenched and spoiled the laden branches of the cultivated wattles—the golden-hued Cootamundra and the earlier Queensland—their paler sisters in the neighbouring bush have survived the downpour, and are shedding their nutty sweetness through a damp world, and the air is fragrant with early spring scents.

This afternoon there was actually a break in the grey sky, and a wind that seemed as if it might blow the rain away. The house grows unsupportable after a whole seven days of rain, and I felt I must go out into the freshness and green. So with old hat, short skirt, and strong high boots I started off along the muddy road to see what the week's rain had brought forth. On the upper part of the ridge the soil is shale, and here grow tall blue gums and iron barks, with grassy spreads beneath them. In the autumn this grass is a great hunting-ground for mushrooms, but now as I trudged across the soppy sods there was nothing but green on every side. All green it was, but not all grass; for at the very edge of the little creek, which was rushing along in muddy haste, I found a group of green orchids —those quaint delicate things with much-curved petals that look so like a strange bird's head. There were two sorts, one

with a single flower on the end of a tall stalk, the other with
several similar though much smaller blossoms on the slender
stem.   Close by, the faint pink of a different orchid glowed
softly, all three together making a dainty bunch.

Last week the bed of the creek was quite dry, but now a
perfect river rushes along, drowning beneath its torrent the bright
green herring-bone ferns which make a glade of greenery all the
year round.   Last week, too, I watched a tomtit bringing food to
his mate as she sat in her nest in a small turpentine overhanging
the creek, and I spied on a pair of blackcaps as they carried fine
twigs to the making of their cradle nest in the highest branch of a
much taller turpentine.   To-day, as I neared the group of dark-
leaved trees, two tomtits flew past with much agitation, the little
golden backs gleaming brightly, and I guessed that there was no
longer need for the mother bird to sit; for as the tomtits are about
the first birds of all to build, the babies would be hatched.   The
little family had survived the long wet week, and now the parents
were taking advantage of the fine spell to catch some tasty insects
for the wee things.   But the blackcaps had been outdone by the
weather, and a few solitary threads were all that remained of the
cradle.   Overhead, amongst the topmast branches a number of
the beautiful things darted, chattering and scolding, and probably
looking for likely spots to hang their nests.   The blackcap is
one of the prettiest of all the honey-eaters, with back of bright
olive, breast of snowy white, a rich, black head, white nape, and
above his eyes a patch of bright vermilion.   He generally chooses

the turpentine for his nesting tree, and hangs his little nest in the highest outermost bunch of leaves.

Last week when the creek was dry two diamond birds, or

Diamond-bird ~ *Pardalotus punctatus*

diamond dicks, as the children call them, were burrowing in the upper bank. There seemed little hope of their work remaining after all this rain, but it is always just as well to look, so I turned my steps towards the spot. To my surprise as I approached, the male bird, a pretty little chap with spotted wings and head, darted out from the bank a foot or so above the stream. Fate had been kind, and the water had not reached the upper bank, where, at the end of the foot-long burrow, a little nest would soon hold a clutch of small white eggs.

The rain was still holding off, so I crossed the creek by a fallen tree, and almost immediately found myself on the sandstone country. Instantly the features of the bush were altered; the blue gums, ironbarks, and turpentines gave way to scribbly gums and banksias, beneath which grew in thick profusion all the prickly, spiky things which make real bush. Three kinds of wattle I found in a minute—the myrtle-leafed, the sweet-scented, and the fine-leafed—and their drying flowers were full of sweetness. Growing beneath the shelter of the small banksias and other thick shrubs were clumps and clumps of the deep pink boronia in full bloom, the starry blossoms quite unspoiled by the rain; but the dillwynia, which should be painting the whole ground gold, bent, sad and pale, its drenched blossoms beneath the clinging raindrops; and faded, too, by the excessive rain were the red spider-flowers, usually so gay and bright in the later winter months.

A breath of nutty fragrance told of the presence of the little whitebeard, and I saw it sheltering beneath the thicker plants, the white of its open flower contrasting prettily with the soft red of its unfolded bud. All through the bush the needlebush

showed white blossoms amongst its spiky leaves, and in one
tree I found a redhead's nest quite within reach.   I approached
it very gingerly—for the needlebush lives well up to its name—
and after a few scratches, one right down my chin, I managed
to put my hand on to the retort-shaped bundle, and tilting it
gently, rolled out five eggs.   Pure white they should have been;
but they were so stained and discoloured that I knew at once
they were addled, and the nest bore signs that the birds had
been using it as a resting-place in the wet weather.   Evidently it
had been deserted by its rightful owners, and other birds had
taken possession, using it as a storm shelter—a fate which often
befalls the redhead's nest.

Amongst the banksias and tea-tree, white-cheeked and New
Holland honey-eaters were noisily feeding and fussing.   They
are both rather showy members of the family, with black-and-
white bodies, and yellow-edged wings, the only marked differ-
ence between them being the broad white fan-shaped tuft of
the white-cheeked honey-eater, from which he gets his name.
Both birds were evidently building, and in a little banksia I
found the nest of the New Holland, with two tiny, hideous,
featherless birds gaping widely for food.   Further on in the heath
close to the ground I found the nest of another honey-eater,
known to science as the tawny-crowned.   An insignificant little
brown bird he is, but with a voice of liquid sweetness, which is to
be heard on the heathlands most months of the year, floating with
a gentle melancholy through the air.

New Holland Honeyeater in *Banksia marginata*

But the find of the afternoon was down by the creek at the bottom of the gully.   There, amongst the thick scrubby bushes I heard the ringing call of the coachwhip bird; and almost immediately by merest accident, in pushing my way through the undergrowth, I stumbled across its nest of loosely joined twigs, wherein lay two eggs of exquisite blue, boldly blotched with sepia spots.   Rare, indeed, is it to find a coachwhip building so early in the year, and to come across a nest with a full set more than repaid me for my long wet walk.   And when upon my homeward way I met the first butterfly of the season, a pretty, bright, brown thing, with black-veined wings, I felt that, despite the rain, which was once more beginning to creep up, spring was indeed well on her way.

FLOWERS BLOOMING.

Ranunculus lappaceus	Buttercup
Hibbertia aspera	
Tetratheca ericifolia	
Zieria laevigata	
Boronia ledifolia	
Boronia polygalifolia	
Correa reflexa	Native fuchsia
Ricinocarpus pinifolius	Native jasmine
Acacia ulicifolia	Juniper-leafed wattle
Acacia suaveolens	Sweet-scented wattle
Acacia myrtifolia	Myrtle-leafed wattle
Acacia longissima	Fine-leafed wattle
Acacia brownii	
Dillwynia retorta	
Bossiaea scolopendria	} Yellow pea-flowers
Cryptandra amara	
Hovea linearis	

Hardenbergia violacea	False sarsaparilla
Melaleuca nodosa	Tea-tree
Baeckea ramosissima	
Darwinia fascicularis	Bread and meat plant
Calytrix tetragona	
Callistemon linearis	} Red bottlebrushes
Callistemon citrinus	
Grevillea speciosa	Red spider-flower
Hakea sericea	Needlebush
Banksia ericifolia	} Honeysuckles, or bottlebrushes
Banksia marginata	
Olearia ramulosa	Snow bush
Pimelea glauca	
Pimelea linifolia	
Astroloma humifusum	} Ground berries
Astroloma pinifolium	
Epacris purpurascens	
Epacris longiflora	Native fuchsia
Epacris microphylla	
Epacris pulchella	
Woollsia pungens	White heath
Leucopogon biflorus	
Leucopogon microphyllus	} Whitebeards
Leucopogon ericoides	
Pterostylis nutans	
Pterostylis reflexa	} Green orchids
Pterostylis longifolia	
Lomandra longifolia	
Lomandra obliqua	
Lomandra multiflora	

BIRDS ARRIVING IN AUGUST.

Hirundo neoxena	Welcome Swallow
Cuculus pallidus	Pallid Cuckoo

BIRDS DEPARTING IN AUGUST.

Anthochaera carunculata	Red Wattlebird

BIRDS BREEDING IN AUGUST.

Corvus coronoides	Australian Raven
Grallina cyanoleuca	Peewee
Colluricincla harmonica	Grey Shrike-thrush
Eopsaltria australis	Eastern Yellow Robin
Malurus cyaneus	Superb Blue Wren
Malurus lamberti	Variegated Wren
Origma solitaria	Rock Warbler
Acanthiza pusilla	Brown Tit or Brown Thornbill
Acanthiza lineata	Striped Tit or Striated Thornbill
Acanthiza chrysorrhoa	Tomtit or Yellow-rumped Thornbill
Acanthiza reguloides	Buff-rumped Thornbill
Psophodes olivaces	Eastern Whipbird
Climacteris picumnus	Brown Treecreeper
Climacteris leucophaea	White-throated Treecreeper
Phylidonyris novaehollandiae	New Holland Honeyeater
Phylidonyris nigra	White-cheeked Honeyeater
Phylidonyris melanops	Tawny-crowned Honeyeater
Lichenostomus melanops	Yellow-tufted Honeyeater
Lichenostomus chrysops	Yellow-faced Honeyeater
Melithreptus lunatus	Blackcap or White-naped Honeyeater
Zosterops lateralis	Silvereye
Pardalotus punctatus	Diamond-bird or Spotted Pardalote
Aegintha temporalis	Red-browed Finch
Anthus novaeseelandiae	Richard's Pipit
Menura novaeseelandiae	Superb Lyrebird
Cuculus pyrrhophanus	Fan-tailed Cuckoo
Chrysococcyx lucidus plagosus	Golden Bronze Cuckoo
Chrysococcyx basalis	Horsfield Bronze Cuckoo

SEPTEMBER

Glossodia major

TO-DAY I found a treasure trove. On the slope of a gentle hill, beneath the shade of young turpentines and sassafras trees, all starred amongst the soft green grass and maidenhair, stood dozens and dozens of the daintiest flowers imaginable, pale mauve and pure white orchids. Their pale faces, lifted skyward on the end of their slender stems, gleamed like stars amongst the short fronds of fern, till a soft wind crept past and set them fluttering like fettered butterflies. Every fairylike blossom sang of spring, and the faint sweet scent which came from them was like an odour from a past September. Too lovely they were to touch, so I just sat and looked at them, and dreamed long dreams—the dreams that always stir and rise as sunny-haired September creeps into the year.

I was not the only dreamer in that beauty spot. A gentle movement in a tree close by caught my eye, and, turning, I saw a yellowbob seated upon her nest. Built on the top of a

broken branch, and ornamented with hanging strips of bark,
it looked so like part of the tree that, but for the slight movement of her tail, I should never have spied the little mother
cuddling down upon her nest.   She knew at once I had seen
her, and her big bright eye watched me suspiciously, but not
another movement did she make until I came quite close to

Viola hederacea

her, then hurriedly she flew off with a little frightened "tchew-
tchew."   I peeped over the edge of the nest, and saw two apple-
green eggs, all spotted with red.   No wonder the little bird
was dreaming so happily, and no wonder she flew away in such
dread at my approach.   But she had no need for fear; I would

Platylobium formosum.

not touch her pretty
treasures. K n o w i n g
that she would not
return while I was near,
I calmed her feelings by
going on my way.

Such a sweet and
flower-decked way it
was, too. All amongst
the undergrowth grew
the bright yellow pea-
flowers of the platy-
lobium, with its pretty
sarsaparilla-like leaves,
myriads of bees droning
amongst the blossoms;
where the trees were
fewer, "snow bushes"
g r e w w h i t e, t h e i r
slender branches massed
with myriads of dainty
white daisy flowers.
On the grass beside
them the yellow orchids,
which children here call
cowslips, showed in the

clearings, while among the tangles of turpentines and gum-suckers two or three different wattles and a whitebeard wafted sweetness abroad.

There were other sweets amongst those same small turpentines. In one, quite close to the ground, I found the nest of a white-cheeked honey-eater; a cosy little home it was, carefully made of fibres, and lined warmly with the soft brown velvet of the banksias. Resting on the rich lining were two exquisite eggs of a delicate pinky cream, with a zone of red spots—a marking characteristic of honey-eater's eggs. Quite close, in another turpentine, I found a similar nest, but this time in place of the eggs were two bare tiny chicks. As soon as I drew near the mother bird came up scolding and chattering furiously, with her fine white tufts puffed out in fear and anger. Evidently she was not able to recognise a friend, so I moved away, and from a little distance watched her fly down to the infants with a tender, anxious cry.

Suddenly above her voice came a sharp bird note, the voice of the spine-billed honey-eater. "Quick, quick, be quick," he called as he flew past, his gun-blue back shining in the sun. "Quick, quick, hurry up, hurry up, quick, quick, quick," called his mate, and she too darted past with loud wing-beat. I followed through the bushes, and after watching their movements for a while saw one fly up with a fibre in his long sharp beak. I crept nearer, and there, in the highest branch of a turpentine sapling, hung an almost finished cradle. It was well out of my reach, so I did not attempt to see closer.

But very soon I came across a nest into which I could easily see. Through the bushes came a faint, sibilant note, which I recognised at once as that of the chestnut-shouldered wren, a rarer cousin of our garden friend, the blue wren. Very still I stood, and waited patiently, gazing in the direction of the cry. Nearer and nearer it came, and suddenly only a few yards in front of me there hopped out a tiny brown mouse-like bird, with a long blue tail held very erect. It was the female, and in her beak she carried a long thread of grass. With hops and jerks she came through the bushes, and then with a flutter made towards a clump of grass almost within my reach, but hidden from sight by a thick sapling. Just for a second she stayed, then was off, but without the thread. I peeped round the sapling, and there, almost on the ground, was her little bulky nest of grass, with its side entrance carefully hidden by the protecting grasses. The nest was almost finished and ready for eggs. The common blue wrens have been a little quicker with their building, for last week I found their nest with two eggs, half the full set.

A sharp "twit-twit-twit" sounded in my ear, and I turned quickly in time to see a small greenish-brown bird flash past. It was the little brown tit, and in his beak he carried a small morsel of food. I followed him quietly and watched him dart for a moment into a small bush and then out again, and away. I stepped up to the spot and there came across one of the tragedies of the bush. In amongst the branches was set a small

Chestnut-shouldered Wren

oval nest, with a doorway at the side, and at this doorway was a sad little sight, of which I had often heard but had never seen with my own eyes. Hanging by its slender claws to the grass threads of the nest, lay the dead body of a tiny baby tit, while on the ground below lay another small body. Inside the nest, where the two baby tits should have been safely hidden, was huddled a bulky young fantail cuckoo, who opened his wide yellow bill, and peeked hungrily at me. He was not sorry for the poor infants he had tumbled out to their death; all he cared for was to get enough to eat, and he squawked and squawked, while the two small foster parents worked their hardest to satisfy his voracious appetite.

But fascinating as the forest country was, I knew that a wealth of beauty was awaiting me; so I pushed on down the hill, across the creek, and up on to the sandstone. As I passed the creek a diamond-bird flew by to a hole in the bank, and by the cheeping and squeaking that came from within I knew there were three or four baby birds in the cosy nest at the end of the tunnel. I did not linger long near this little strange home, for the blaze of colour ahead lured me on. Surely there was never anything more beautiful than that stretch of bush, which but a few weeks before had been bare and unlovely. Now it shone and shimmered with a wealth of flowers of every colour and shape. Spring had flung her gold with a prodigal hand, and the yellow pea-flowers of the dillwynia, the pultenaea, and the aotus gleamed like tiny fairy sovereigns, while lower

down on the sand the gold and rich brown flowers of the
bossiaea shone on their quaint, flat, leafless stems. Pale in
comparison to the gorgeous pea blossoms were the lemon-yellow
flower spikes of the lemon-scented phebalium, which grew near
the creek, and even the golden balls of the juniper-leafed wattle
paled before their brilliancy. But here was another flower which
vied with them in gorgeousness; it was the deep pink boronia,
which spread like a flowing carpet on every hand. A week ago
it was at its height of glory; now, it is just on its wane, though
still full of beauty. But in a few more weeks it will make way
for its paler sister. Amongst the boronia, the lysinema lifted tall,
sweet, white spikes, and three other epacrids lent softness to the
colour scheme, while close by a regular mass of white-beards in
full bloom shed an intoxicating sweetness and fascinated hundreds of bees to their midst. Another sweet-scented flower I
found was logania, a shrub with small creamy bell flowers, growing near the creek.

Then up on the heathlands I came across a host of
sprengelia, one of the epacris family, whose thick, pink heads
of star-blossoms stand straight up amongst the brown grass
or green bead fern. It is always found in the heath, especially
in the swampy parts, and is very plentiful near Long Bay and
Maroubra. Up on those same highlands last week I found the
first native rose (Boronia serrulata), and also the first hibbertia
—a golden blossom very like a small dog-rose. There, too,

I found an eriostemon in flower, with its pale pink starry blossoms gleaming like tiny camelias against its silvery stems and long leaves. This flower is one of our best spring bloomers, and with its sister, the box-leafed eriostemon, is very plentiful along the coast.

Eriostemon buxifolius

There is one flower which it is not necessary to go further than the train window to see, and that is the hardenbergia. Just at present it is wrapping all the cuttings in its regal coat of purple; it streams over the red clay, creeps through the green grass, clambers over old logs and fences, and even climbs into the branches of small trees. Sometimes it is accompanied by its less conspicuous friend, the tecoma, that creeper with creamy red-spotted bells, which make soft masses of bloom over fences and tree trunks. The white wax stars of the wild clematis also shine out of the grass of the railway embankments, or festoon with bridal wreaths the tree-trunks in the brush.

It is, indeed, a time of sweetness in sight and scent and sound. The air is everywhere fragrant with perfume, the eyes are gladdened on every side by gorgeous blossoms, and as for the sounds—the world is full of them. It is quite impossible to sleep these mornings, for at daybreak begins the bird chorus, led always by the Jacky Winter, whose "peter, peter, peter," is one of the first bird notes to greet the morn. Even through the night the birds are not silent. Last night I heard two cuckoos calling all through the hours

Clematis aristata

of darkness; the wail of the bronze cuckoo was answered again and again by the rollicking note of the pallid cuckoo, the one of his family who seems least oppressed by his fate. Now is the time of all times for one to peep into the mysteries of the bush, and those who have not yet read from the magic pages of Nature's book will find no better season for opening the cover than sweet September.

FLOWERS BLOOMING.

Clematis glycinoides
Hibbertia aspera
Hibbertia fasciculata
Hibbertia linearis
Hibbertia dentata
Viola hederacea
Viola betonicifolia
Pittosporum undulatum
Pittosporum revolutum
Drosera pygmaea   Sundew, flycatcher
Tetratheca ericifolia
Zieria laevigata
Zieria pilosa
Zieria smithii
Boronia ledifolia
Boronia pinnata
Boronia floribunda
Boronia serrulata   Native rose
Correa alba
Correa reflexa   Native fuchsia
Philotheca salsolifolia
Phebalium dentatum
Phebalium squamulosum
Eriostemon buxifolius

Eriostemon australasius	
Rulingia hermanniifolia	
Ricinocarpus pinifolius	Native jasmine
Mirbelia rubiifolia	
Acacia baileyana	Cootamundra wattle
Acacia decurrens	Green wattle
Acacia ulicifolia	Juniper-leafed wattle
Acacia brownii	
Acacia longifolia	Sydney golden wattle
Acacia floribunda	
Acacia myrtifolia	Myrtle-leafed wattle
Acacia stricta	
Sphaerolobium vimineum	
Pultenaea stipularis	
Pultenaea daphnoides	
Phyllota phyllicoides	
Dillwynia retorta	
Dillwynia floribunda	Yellow pea-flowers
Dillwynia juniperina	
Platylobium formosum	
Bossiaea scolopendria	
Daviesia genistifolia	
Aotus ericoides	
Hovea linearis	
Indigofera australis	Native indigo
Hardenbergia violacea	False sarsaparilla
Bauera rubioides	Wild dog-rose
Melaleuca nodosa	Tea-tree
Baeckea ramosissima	
Calytrix tetragona	
Leptospermum laevigatum	
Leptospermum scoparium	Tea-trees
Leptospermum attenuatum	
Callistemon citrinus	Red bottlebrush
Cryptandra amara	
Petrophila pulchella	
Isopogon anethifolius	Drum stick

Telopea speciosissima	Waratah
Conospermum texifolia	
Grevillea speciosa	Red spider-flower
Grevillea buxifolia	Grey spider-flower
Grevillea linearifolia	White spider-flower
Grevillea sericea	Pink spider-flower
Grevillea mucronulata	Green spider-flower
Hakea teretifolia	} Needlebushes
Hakea sericea	
Banksia ericifolia	} Honeysuckles, or bottlebrushes
Banksia marginata	
Olearia ramulosa	Snow bush
Goodenia hederacea	
Logonia albiflora	
Mitrasacme polymorpha	
Pimelea glauca	
Pimelea linifolia	
Utricularia lateriflora	Bladderwort
Pandorea pandorana	
Brachyloma daphnoides	
Astroloma humifusum	Ground berries
Epacris longiflora	Native fuchsia

Hibbertia scandens   *Phebalium squamulosum*

Epacris obtusifolia
Epacris microphylla
Epacris pulchella
Woollsia pungens   White heath
Sprengelia incarnata
Leucopogon amplexicaulis
Leucopogon lanceolatus   } Whitebeards
Leucopogon parviflorus
Leucopogon ericoides
Styphelia tubiflora
Styphelia triflora   } Five-corners
Styphelia longifolia
Calochilus paludosus
Diuris punctata
Diuris maculata
Diuris sulphurea
Caladenia carnea
Caladenia alba   } Orchids
Caladenia filamentosa
Caleana major
Prasophyllum elatum
Glossodia major
Glossodia minor

Dillwynia retorta

Pultenaea daphnoides

Thelymitra ixioides	Wild ixia
Pterostylis obtusa	Greenhood
Pterostylis nutans	Parrot-beak orchid
Dendrobium speciosum	Rock lily
Burchardia umbellata	Milkmaids
Sowerbaea juncea	
Stypandra caespitosa	

BIRDS ARRIVING IN SEPTEMBER.

Lalage sueurii	White-winged Triller
Gerygone olivacea	Native Canary or White-throated Warbler
Pachycephala rufiventris	Rufous-breasted Thickhead or Rufous Whistler
Myzomela sanguinolenta	Scarlet Honeyeater
Halcyon sanctus	Sacred Kingfisher

BIRDS BREEDING IN SEPTEMBER.

Corvus coronoides	Australian Raven
Grallina cyanoleuca	Peewee
Colluricincla harmonica	Grey Shrike-thrush
Lalage sueurii	White-winged Triller
Rhipidura fuliginosa	Grey Fantail
Rhipidura leucophrys	Willie Wagtail
Myiagra inquieta	Razor Grinder or Restless Flycatcher
Microeca leucophaea	Jacky Winter or Brown Flycatcher
Gerygone olivacea	Native Canary or White-throated Warbler
Eopsaltria australis	Eastern Yellow Robin
Malurus cyaneus	Superb Blue Wren
Malurus lamberti	Variegated Wren
Dacelo novaeguineae	Laughing Kookaburra

Cuculus pallidus	Pallid Cuckoo
Cuculus pyrrhophanus	Fan-tailed Cuckoo
Chrysococcyx lucidus plagosus	Golden Bronze Cuckoo
Chrysococcyx basalis	Horsfield Bronze Cuckoo
Turnix varia	Painted Quail
Cisticola exilis	Golden-headed Cisticola
Acanthiza pusilla	Brown Tit or Brown Thornbill
Acanthiza nana	Little Thornbill
Acanthiza chrysorrhoa	Tomtit or Yellow-rumped Thornbill
Acanthiza lineata	Striped Tit or Striated Thornbill
Psophodes olivaces	Eastern Whipbird
Ephthianura albifrons	White-fronted Chat
Cracticus torquatus	Grey Butcherbird
Pachycephala pectoralis	Yellow-breasted Thickhead or Golden Whistler
Pachycephala rufiventris	Rufous-breasted Thickhead or Rufous Whistler
Falcunculus frontatus	Shrike-tit
Climacteris picumnus	Brown Treecreeper
Climacteris leucophaea	White-throated Treecreeper
Neositta chrysoptera	Orange-winged Sittella
Phylidonyris novaehollandiae	New Holland Honeyeater
Phylidonyris nigra	White-cheeked Honeyeater
Phylidonyris melanops	Tawny-crowned Honeyeater
Lichenostomus chrysops	Yellow-faced Honeyeater
Myzomela sanguinolenta	Scarlet Honeyeater
Melithreptus lunatus	Blackcap or White-naped Honeyeater
Zosterops lateralis	Silvereye
Pardalotus punctatus	Diamond-bird or Spotted Pardalote
Hirundo neoxena	Welcome Swallow
Artamus cyanopterus	Dusky Woodswallow
Anthus novaeseelandiae	Richard's Pipit
Podargus strigoides	Morepork or Tawny Frogmouth

OCTOBER

Boronia serrulata

Q UITE early last month the pittosporum came out and scented the world with its sweetness. It streamed t h r o u g h gardens and along roads, vieing with the stocks and freesias in beauty, and for a week or so the nights were intoxicating with its perfume. It is over now in the gardens; and in the bush, its native sphere, only a stray blossom remains to tell of the glory that has passed. But though the pittosporum has had its day and vanished, there is still a long succession of sweetness to greet the senses at every stage. The heavier-scented white-blossomed plants, such as the whitebeards and logania, are almost over, but the real bush-sweet, aromatic scents have taken their place. Up on the highlands there is a perfume which, if you met it in the farthest corner of the earth, would carry you straight back to Sydney on a sunny day. It is not of any particular flower or tree, but of dozens and dozens of them, all mixed up together, blossoms and leaves, and the smell of the earth; and it is a scent that brings freshness and health with it, clears the brain, and makes you throw back your head with a smile of content.

It is a scent that drags you willy-nilly out into the bush,
and as Monday was a whole free day, and the sun was bright,
I took my bag and billy, and went out to enjoy the delights.
And, oh, such a day I had! Ten minutes after leaving the railway line I was in bush as thick and real as if it were miles from
any city.   A rough cart-track crawled white and dusty through
the scrub; but even in the ruts grew flowers—blue dampiera,
yellow goodenia, and a tall brown orchid, almost indistinguish-
able from the grass around it.   Along the sides of the track
stretched dwarf apple (with red velvety buds, which in a little
while will break into a mass of creamy blossoms), and stunted
gums and tea-trees. Beneath the shelter of the bushes gleamed
in rosy masses the paler boronia—the deep pink one has entirely
vanished—and the clumps of a pale mauve star-flower, philotheca.

A little further on the dwarf apples and saplings gave way to
taller scribbly gums beneath whose shelter one of the dillwynias
raised golden spikes, while a pultenaea sent up great heads of
still deeper gold to outshine it in gorgeousness.   Beyond the
gums stretched the marsh which a month ago was a carpet of
pink sprengelia, now snowy white with the tubular-flowered
epacris, sweetest of all the heaths, and the conospermum, whose
flower heads, mostly unfavourably known as the centre pieces
of stiff bunches, wave gracefully on long slender stems in their
natural surroundings.

But it was where the track ran round the side of the hill

that the sweetest flowers were found. Against the grey rocks
huge bushes of bauera, the native dog-rose, stretched feathery
pink-laden sprays, and tall, white tea-trees made a happy hunting-ground for numerous small, shining beetles.   And, lower

Maidenhair fern

down, sheltered from sun and wind, grew a whole treasure trove
of that most prized flower, the palest pink boronia, which at
present is glorifying the street baskets.   In a few minutes my

hands were as full as they would hold of the feathery beauty.
At least, I thought so, till I spied the deeper pink of still another
boronia, the native rose, which was scattered profusely over the
grey sand. Then such a bunch I gathered of the two together,
and it was only when I was absolutely unable to hold another stalk
that I could tear myself away.

But there were more joys awaiting me. At the point I had
decided on as my destination I came upon a sight that was
more like a scene from a fairy book than a bit of Australian
bush. On the top of a little knoll is a group of tall she-oaks
whose needles, undisturbed for years, have made a soft, brown
carpet beneath the trees; and to-day, growing in every
direction across this carpet, were hundreds of lobelias, their
bright blue, delicate blossoms swaying gently at the faintest
breath. Here, resting on the fragrant carpet, I ate my lunch;
and never did hard-boiled eggs taste better, though it seemed
almost a sacrilege to bring such mundane things into such
surroundings.

On my way home I came round by the creek, and there
I simply had to gather another bunch of flowers, for no one
could have resisted the gorgeousness of the gompholobium—
alas the name!—with its huge pea-flowers of purest yellow.
The whole creek was lined with gold, for one of the pultenaeas
stretched long, yellow, flower-laden sprays a dozen feet into
the air, and shed sweetness everywhere on the hillside. I also
found masses of the dainty mauve creeper comesperma, which

has taken the place of the hardenbergia, now departed, and I had to add it to the yellow bunch.

Fortunately for my poor hands, I did not come across any waratahs or rock lilies, though they are out in all their glory at present. But it is quite impossible to pass empty-handed through the bush these days, for spring has been painting the world with a lavish brush since early August, and September and October are most gorgeous of all months for flower treasures.

Comesperma volubile

September has been a busy time for the birds, too. A fortnight ago I found the tiniest nest I have ever seen. I was watching a lovely little red-headed honey-eater—that beautiful scarlet and black bird, familiarly known as the blood-bird—feeding busily in the top of a small turpentine tree, only ceasing operations now and again to utter his little running call. This was answered from higher up the hill, and presently his small brown mate came hurrying into the tree, and commenced to weave a bark fibre into her tiny cradle, which was quite invisible until she drew my attention to it. It was not much bigger than a half-crown, and so thinly built that a week later I could plainly see the two tiny eggs through the bottom of the nest. These last were creamy white, with a zone of brownish spots round the top, and are so small as to make it almost incredible that they can ever hold little birds within their shell.

The eggs are something like, though smaller than, those of the little grey fantail, which is also nesting now. I know two nests, both like wineglasses with the foot broken off, neatly covered with grey-white cobweb, and both now containing eggs. The square-tailed cuckoo generally places her egg in the fantail's nest; but this parasitic lady only arrived last Saturday. so my fantails have escaped her imposition. The square-tailed has the funniest note of all the cuckoos. The bird begins quite quietly, but seems to work up into a state of excitement, and the song ends in an incoherent high-pitched whistle. The whole sounds something like, "We're going to work, we're going to work, we're going to work, we're going to—we are, we are, we are." And they go to work quickly, too; as I shall show you.

Last month I was pleased to have found a nest of the chestnut-shouldered wren, first cousin to our common blue wren. Pleased, because the bird is rather rare, and the nest is always hard to find. Last month's nest now contains a family. On Saturday last I came across another nest, the owners of which have not been quite so fortunate; I was down the gully—where I had flushed a thrush from her beautifully-situated bark nest, placed in a little cavity in the charred hollow of an old tree, and was peeping at her pearly treasures, with their spots of slate and brown—when a male wren came hurrying across the creek, and flew straight to a dead bush lying on the ground, from which a larger bird came away, the little wren following in indignant pur-

Gum tips

suit.   I saw that the big bird was the square-tailed cuckoo, which had only arrived that very day, and walked over to the bush to see the cause of the fuss.   I at once saw the wrens' nest, and beneath it, on the ground, were two unbroken eggs, which the cuckoo had evidently turned out.   No wonder Mr. Wren was indignant.   I did not interfere, as I wanted to see whether the cuckoo would place her own egg in the nest, but on returning two days later, found the third egg had been turned out.   I suppose the cuckoo was not ready to lay, and wanted to start the wrens afresh, so that they could have a

Fantail on nest

nest prepared by the time she was ready.   Cuckoos are given to cool habits of this kind.

Other birds which have returned from their northward flight are the kingfisher and the native canary. All day long the running liquid notes of the latter sounds amid the saplings, and I know of a nest just ready for lining.   The thickheads, those sweet songsters, are building, too, and their fibre nests are seen in several tea-trees, while a pair of kookaburras are busy tunnelling into an ants' nest in a tree down in the next paddock.   It is the busiest month in the year, and the time when anyone who wants to know the birds can easily become acquainted with them.

FLOWERS BLOOMING.

Hibbertia aspera	
Hibbertia linearis	
Hibbertia dentata	
Viola betonicifolia	Wild violet
Hybanthus monopetalus	Winged violet
Tetratheca ericifolia	
Zieria pilosa	
Zieria laevigata	
Drosera pygmaoea	
Drosera binata	} Sundews, flycatchers
Comesperma volubile	
Comesperma ericinum	
Boronia pinnata	
Boronia floribunda	
Boronia serrulata	Native rose
Correa alba	
Correa reflexa	Native fuchsia
Philotheca salsolifolia	
Eriostemon buxifolius	
Eriostemon australasius	
Eriostemon scaber	
Lasiopetalum ferrugineum	Rusty petals
Ricinocarpus pinifolius	Native jasmine
Poranthera ericifolia	
Poranthera corymbosa	

Dodonaea triquetra	Hopbush
Gompholobium grandiflorum	
Indigofera australis	
Phyllota phyllicoides	
Pultenaea daphnoides	
Pultenaea retusa	
Pultenaea villosa	Yellow pea-flowers
Pultenaea flexilis	
Dillwynia retorta	
Dillwynia floribunda	
Callicoma serratifolia	Black wattle
Bauera rubioides	Wild dog-rose
Bauera capitata	
Kunzea ambigua	
Kunzea capitata	
Darwinia fascicularis	Bread and meat plant
Leptospermum laevigatum	Tea-trees
Leptospermum scoparium	
Callistemon citrinus	Red bottlebrush
Pomaderris lanigera	
Pomaderris elliptica	
Olax stricta	
Grevillea speciosa	Red spider-flower
Grevillea buxifolia	Grey spider-flower
Telopea speciosissima	Waratah
Conospermum ericifolium	
Lobelia dentata	
Lobelia gracilis	
Dampiera purpurea	
Dampiera stricta	
Scaevola ramosissima	
Goodenia ovata	
Goodenia hederacea	
Utricularia lateriflora	Bladderwort
Prostanthera marifolia	
Prostanthera sieberi	
Hemigenia purpurea	
Westringia fruticosa	Wild rosemary

Chloanthes stoechadis
Epacris obtusifolia
Epacris microphylla
Epacris pulchella
Dendrobium speciosum   Rock lily
Galeola cassythoides
Calochilus paludosus
Diuris aurea
Diuris punctata   } Orchids
Caleana major
Microtis unifolia
Patersonia fragilis
Patersonia glabrata
Doryanthes excelsa   Gigantic lily
Stypandra caespitosa
Dianella caerulea
Dianella laevis

BIRDS ARRIVING IN OCTOBER.

Myiagra rubecula	Leaden Flycatcher
Cuculus variolosus	Square-tailed or Brush Cuckoo

BIRDS BREEDING IN OCTOBER.

Corvus coronoides	Australian Raven
Grallina cyanoleuca	Peewee
Colluricincla harmonica	Grey Shrike-thrush
Lalage sueurii	White-winged Triller
Rhipidura fuliginosa	Grey Fantail
Rhipidura leucophrys	Willie Wagtail
Myiagra inquieta	Razor Grinder or Restless Flycatcher
Microeca leucophaea	Jacky Winter or Brown Flycatcher
Gerygone olivacea	Native Canary or White-throated Warbler
Eopsaltria australis	Eastern Yellow Robin
Malurus cyaneus	Suberb Blue Wren
Malurus lamberti	Variegated Wren
Origma solitaria	Rock Warbler
Cisticola exilis	Golden-headed Cisticola

Acanthiza pusilla	Brown Tit or Brown Thornbill
Acanthiza nana	Little Thornbill
Acanthiza lineata	Striped Tit or Striated Thornbill
Acanthiza chrysorrhoa	Tomtit or Yellow-rumped Thornbill
Acanthiza reguloides	Buff-rumped Thornbill
Psophodes olivaces	Eastern Whipbird
Ephthianura albifrons	White-fronted Chat
Cracticus torquatus	Grey Butcherbird
Pachycephala pectoralis	Yellow-breasted Thickhead or Golden Whistler
Pachycephala rufiventris	Rufous-breasted Thickhead or Rufous Whistler
Falcunculus frontatus	Shrike-tit
Climacteris picumnus	Brown Treecreeper
Climacteris leucophaea	White-throated Treecreeper
Neositta chrysoptera	Orange-winged Sittella
Phylidonyris novaehollandiae	New Holland Honeyeater
Phylidonyris melanops	Tawny-crowned Honeyeater
Lichenostomus chrysops	Yellow-faced Honeyeater
Lichenostomus melanops	Yellow-tufted Honeyeater
Acanthorhynchus tenuirostris	Eastern Spinebill
Myzomela sanguinolenta	Scarlet Honeyeater
Melithreptus lunatus	Blackcap or White-naped Honeyeater
Zosterops lateralis	Silvereye
Pardalotus punctatus	Diamond-bird or Spotted Pardalote
Hirundo neoxena	Welcome Swallow
Artamus cyanopterus	Dusky Woodswallow
Aegintha temporalis	Red-browed Finch
Anthus novaeseelandiae	Richard's Pipit
Podargus strigoides	Morepork or Tawny Frogmouth
Dacelo novaeguineae	Laughing Kookaburra
Halcyon sanctus	Sacred Kingfisher
Cuculus pallidus	Pallid Cuckoo
Cuculus pyrrhophanus	Fan-tailed Cuckoo
Cuculus variolosus	Square-tailed or Brush Cuckoo
Chrysococcyx lucidus plagosus	Golden Bronze Cuckoo
Chrysococcyx basalis	Horsfield Bronze Cuckoo
Turnix varia	Painted Quail

NOVEMBER

I T was two butterflies that did the mischief to-day. I had quite made up my mind to have a nice day's sewing, and had planned two blouses to be made; but while I sat at breakfast on the verandah those blue butterflies came floating by, and the blouses were forgotten. In and out amongst the red tips of the gum-saplings they flittered, living turquoise in a frame of burnished copper. A little wind, too young to be rough, flittered softly after them and set the red leaves dancing as it passed. Some sunbeams, seeing the dancing leaves, came to join in the fun, and butterflies, leaves, and sunbeams danced and sparkled together in the soft sweet breeze.

It was irresistible. I set down my coffee cup and stood up. "It's no use," I said to myself, "no one could be expected to sit still and sew

to-day, when all the world's a-dancing.   It is a day for the
bush!" So off to the bush I went.

The butterflies danced off before me to show me the way.
Down the hill they went, where a grass-covered slope runs
to the creek. The hillside was a-dancing, too, with the quiver-
ing shivery grass, and the blue wings fluttered daintily over
the feathery, waving mass.   To the creek they led me, where
the young fronds of the herring-bone ferns shone red against
the vivid green of the older fronds.   I stopped a minute to
gaze into their funnily-curled tips and touch their soft hairy
stems.   When I looked up again the butterflies had gone. Perhaps they had flown on to entice someone else out to the trees
and grass.   I was sorry to lose the beautiful things, but I no
longer needed their guidance. They had shown me the way and I
would find the rest for myself.

The question was not which way to go, but which way not
to go, for something called on every side.   Just behind me as
I stood came a running stream of song, sweet and clear.   It
was the voice of the native canary sitting in the lower
branches of a small gum, only a few yards from me; with the
morning sun on his bright yellow breast and small white
throat, he more than rivalled his namesake in colour and
sweetness.   Near him, on a small twig sat his little mate,
with wings outspread, busily preening herself. They did not
move as I stepped towards them, but, even when I found their
little nest hanging in the sapling beneath them, went on quite

unconcernedly with their occupations, he with his song and she with her toilet. Such a cosy little home it was, with its little side door covered by an overhanging roof. I rolled it gently over, and out into the palm of my hand rolled one, two, three pink-spotted eggs. Now the little mistress bird showed signs of agitation, though not of alarm; but master went on unconcernedly with his song. I did not want to harass the dear things' feelings, so I quickly put the eggs back into their hiding place; and I hope that in a little while I shall have the joy of seeing three baby birds' faces peeping out from the tiny porch.

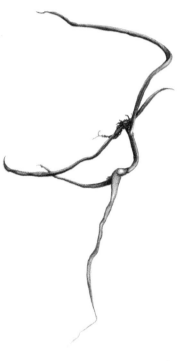

"Cree-cree-cree" went a harsh, shrill note, as a gleam of turquoise flashed through the trees.   It was the note of the sacred kingfisher, as he flew down the creek to a big old red gum. Here, half-way to the top, jutted out a knobby white ants'

Kunzea ambigua

nest, to which the kingfisher darted, and I knew that within lay a clutch of pure white eggs. For the birds came down from the north more than a month ago, and have been busy building since their arrival. A little while they will stay with us, nesting and bringing out their young, brightening the bush with their gay plumage, and deafening our ears with their loud voices. Then, early in the year, before the first cold days of autumn have arrived, they will be off again on their northward flight.

In another red gum not far off I found a second bird breeding in a white ants' nest. It was our friend the kookaburra, who is also a kingfisher. He must have had some difficulty in making up his mind where to nest, for the red gum branches were full of the most alluring spouts, which must have been hard to resist. For the kookaburra, as well as the sacred kingfisher, is just as fond of a spout as of a white ants' nest, and when he finds both together it must be rather hard to choose between them However, the white ants' nest had it this time, and soon there will be some new little kookaburras to join their voices to the laughing morning chorus.

Already the bush is a-twitter with baby voices, and parent birds are kept very busy finding food for the hungry ones. As I walked along the creek I saw a little grey bird running head first down the trunk of a stringy bark, and peering into every crack and crevice as he went. It was the little tree-runner, who always gets his food in this manner. He flies to the top of a tree, works carefully downwards, poking his pointed, upturned bill into every cranny until he reaches the ground, then flies off to another top, to repeat the performance. I watched him working busily for a while, till his industry was rewarded by a nice fat grub, which he immediately carried off to a branch above and killed. Then, with the grub in his beak, he flew away, showing a band of rich orange on his outstretched wings. Away he went to the top of a high tree, where in the fork of a withered branch was placed one of the neatest nests in all the bush, and one of the hardest to see, so cunningly was it wrought out of spiders' webs and cocoons, and an outer covering of bark which made it look like a continuation of the branch.

But even the most carefully disguised nest does not deceive the small boy; the yellow robin's nest is quite as cleverly made to look like its surroundings as is the tree-runner's, and yet it is one of the nests most often the prey of the young savages. All through the bush here are the yellowbobs, and early in the season I found their nests again and again within hand reach; but, alas, the small boy always finds them, too, and now in desperation the birds have taken to building quite high in the trees, and from a branch ever so far above me the big bright eyes of a Mrs. Yellowbob looked down at me with suspicion, as she snuggled down on her treasures, though by this time she should have been feeding fledglings. But, in spite of the ravaging small boy, there are dozens and dozens of

Lambertia formosa

young birds abroad. On one twig, nestling closely together for support, sat a family of three diamond-birds, squawking hungrily for the food which their parents brought them in turns. Young honey-eaters are everywhere; spinebills, New Hollands, and white-cheeked, all with their characteristic beaks and flight, but still lacking the brighter plumage of the adult birds. In a bursaria bush I found Mr. and Mrs. Blue Wren, busily feeding young ones; such fluffy little brown balls they were, too, with absurdly long tails sticking up very straight. By and by some of them will blossom forth in the gorgeous blue and black suit of the father bird, but at present they all wear the safe and sombre brown of their mother.

In the branches of a turpentine I came across an infant who was not so happy as the blue wrens and diamonds-birds. It was a big, fluffed-out baby pallid cuckoo, who sat dismally bunched on a branch wailing miserably while a fierce war was waged around him. Evidently it was time for him to declare himself in his true colours, for his rightful parents kept flying

round and round the tree, calling loudly as they went. The
foster parent, a blackcap, was wild with rage and fear; again
and again she dashed at and in her fury drove away the cuckoos,
who were many times her size. But although they would retreat
before her onslaught, it was only to return with the same calling
note.   And always the baby bird wailed and wailed, as if miser-
able at having to choose.

I watched them for a long time, but the battle seemed to show
no signs of ending, so I passed on, through the fence to the rocky
ground leading down to the river.

The first thing that met my eyes was a bright yellow orchid
creeping in a long strand up the blackened trunk of a burnt
gum.   It hung on its ugly host with tender little arms, which
held it firmly in place, and its delicate flowers stood out vividly

Callistemon citrinus

against the dark background. Most of the orchids are over now, and it was a joy to find such a beauty. Indeed, most of the spring flowers have vanished, and the few hot days of summer have taken much of the colour from those that remain. Here and there a sheltered spray of boronia speaks of past glory, but though the mass of it has vanished, the bush is still pink in patches with the pinkish purple flowers of the kunzea, which spreads all over the sandstone country. The red flowers of lambertia, the honey flower, show up bravely amongst the dark, spiked leaves, and here and there the red bottlebrush (callistemon) lends a dash of colour. But the blaze of colour is past, and it is mostly smaller, quieter flowers that are now in bloom. All through the scrubby undergrowth I found that quaint little creeper billardiera—better known to most of us as "puddings," on account of its fruit, which look like green roly-polies, and have served as dessert for many a dinner in our cubby-house days. At present it is in flower, and its dainty bell-blossoms of pale yellow creep everywhere.

It was right amongst the rocks and sandy patches that I found the best flowers of all, the flannel flowers. Such big, bright stars they were, too, as they gleamed against the dark grey rocks. In a few minutes I had gathered as many as I wanted, and then I turned my face homewards. The sun was burning right above my head now; the birds were silenced by the noonday heat, but the bush was noisy with the hum of flying things, cicadas, moths, and beetles. In the white blossoms of a tea-tree hundreds of pretty blue and green beetles were clustering, their shining wing-cases gleaming like bright enamel. Near the tea-trees grew dwarf apples, rich in velvet buds, with here and there a newly-opened creamy blossom, where bees lurked and drowsed. These red apple buds and the red new leaves of the gum-saplings take the place of the gayer, brighter spring show. I picked a bunch of the shining gum-leaves, and placed them with my flannel flowers; then, because I could not bear to see their beauty fade in the midday heat, I hurried up the hill and home again.

FLOWERS BLOOMING.

Billardiera scandens	Puddings
Pultenaea villosa	} Yellow pea-flowers
Pultenaea flexilis	
Jacksonia scoparia	
Ceratopetalum gummiferum	Christmas bush
Angophora hispida	Dwarf apple
Melaleuca ericifolia	} Tea-trees
Melaleuca styphelioides	
Kunzea capitata	
Leptospermum flavescens	Tea-tree
Callistemon citrinus	Red bottlebrush
Scaevola ramosissima	
Grevillea buxifolia	Grey spider-flower
Actinotus helianthi	Flannel flower
Actinotus minor	Little flannel flower
Lambertia formosa	Honey flower
Galeola cassythoides	
Diuris aurea	
Caleana major	
Dipodium punctatum	
Doryanthes excelsa	Gigantic lily

BIRDS BREEDING IN NOVEMBER.

Corvus coronoides	Australian Raven
Grallina cyanoleuca	Peewee

Flannel flowers - *Actinotus helianthi*

Colluricincla harmonica	Grey Shrike-thrush
Lalage sueurii	White-winged Triller
Rhipidura fuliginosa	Grey Fantail
Rhipidura leucophrys	Willie Wagtail
Myiagra inquieta	Razor Grinder or Restless Flycatcher
Microeca leucophaea	Jacky Winter or Brown Flycatcher
Gerygone olivacea	Native Canary or White-throated Warbler
Eopsaltria australis	Eastern Yellow Robin
Malurus cyaneus	Suberb Blue Wren
Malurus lamberti	Variegated Wren
Origma solitaria	Rock Warbler
Cisticola exilis	Golden-headed Cisticola
Acanthiza pusilla	Brown Tit or Brown Thornbill
Acanthiza nana	Little Thornbill
Acanthiza lineata	Striped Tit or Striated Thornbill
Acanthiza chrysorrhoa	Tomtit or Yellow-rumped Thornbill

Acanthiza reguloides	Buff-rumped Thornbill
Psophodes olivaces	Eastern Whipbird
Ephthianura albifrons	White-fronted Chat
Cracticus torquatus	Grey Butcherbird
Pachycephala pectoralis	Yellow-breasted Thickhead or Golden Whistler
Pachycephala rufiventris	Rufous-breasted Thickhead or Rufous Whistler
Falcunculus frontatus	Shrike-tit
Climacteris picumnus	Brown Treecreeper
Climacteris leucophaea	White-throated Treecreeper
Neositta chrysoptera	Orange-winged Sittella
Phylidonyris novaehollandiae	New Holland Honeyeater
Phylidonyris melanops	Tawny-crowned Honeyeater
Lichenostomus chrysops	Yellow-faced Honeyeater
Lichenostomus melanops	Yellow-tufted Honeyeater
Acanthorhynchus tenuirostris	Eastern Spinebill
Myzomela sanguinolenta	Scarlet Honeyeater
Melithreptus lunatus	Blackcap or White-naped Honeyeater

Billardiera scandens with Silvereye

Zosterops lateralis	Silvereye
Pardalotus punctatus	Diamond-bird or Spotted Pardalote
Hirundo neoxena	Welcome Swallow
Artamus cyanopterus	Dusky Woodswallow
Aegintha temporalis	Red-browed Finch
Anthus novaeseelandiae	Richard's Pipit
Podargus strigoides	Morepork or Tawny Frogmouth
Dacelo novaeguineae	Laughing Kookaburra
Halcyon sanctus	Sacred Kingfisher
Cuculus pallidus	Pallid Cuckoo
Cuculus pyrrhophanus	Fan-tailed Cuckoo
Cuculus variolosus	Square-tailed or Brush Cuckoo
Chrysococcyx lucidus plagosus	Golden Bronze Cuckoo
Chrysococcyx basalis	Horsfield Bronze Cuckoo
Turnix varia	Painted Quail

Tea tree ⌃
Leptospermum flavescens

DECEMBER

THE proper time for a bush walk just now is at five o'clock in the morning; so to-day, while the sun was still flinging long shadows from the east, I was out in the garden ready for my walk. The garden itself was not wanting in charms at that early hour, with the bright faces of pansies smiling in a row, and sweet peas scenting the air. I looked round the beds hesitatingly. There was a good deal of delightful work to be done, and for a moment I wondered if I should not stay.

But only for a moment. A chirping note sounded behind me, and I looked round from the pansies just in time to see a Jacky Winter deposit a nice little moth in the wide-open bill of its baby, who was sitting on my garden fence. With his feathers loosely fluffed, the young bird looked big enough to be taking care of himself, but the mottled head and breast showed that he was still only an infant.

But, though he was only a very young bird, he was quite big enough to make my decision for me. The pansies and the sweet peas were fascinating, but who could stay in an ordinary garden when just a few minutes' walk away was a bush full of fluffy, darling baby birds! Not I. Almost ashamed of the minutes I had already wasted, I hurried through the gate and down the hill into the gully.

Oh, that gully! I almost had to shut my eyes as I came to

it.   Across the clearing, where the grass seems always green, thousands of dandelions held up bright discs to the sun; just beyond, the early light blazed upon the vivid tips of the saplings, now no longer red, but turned to gleaming, burnished copper, and between and above and through all floated hundreds and hundreds of yellow butterflies.   Never have I seen so many; the air was filled with their flittering wings, and as I walked I had to step carefully for fear of crushing them.   Sometimes one would light upon a dead branch on the ground and fold its wings.   Instantly the yellow would disappear, and in its place would be found what looked exactly like a dead brown leaf.   But only a few rested; the others floated here, there, and everywhere, like living sunbeams.   Even in the early morning light the picture was one of golden summer, and after gazing

entranced for a few minutes I hastened instinctively across to the shelter of the trees.

Here I found the things I had come out to see.   All round me sounded the feeble "peeks" and hushed "chirrups" of young birds and their parents.   November and December might be called the "mother" months, so full is the bush just now of baby birds. The loud, gay songs of early

spring are rarely heard now; in their place comes the tender
mother song and baby talk of the fond and anxious parents;
for mother birds have a special tone for their little ones just
as surely as have human mothers, and the voice of the baby bird
is as distinct from its parents' as is the wail of a little baby from
the voice of a woman.

Amongst the leaves around me I knew quite well that some
young things were hiding, and judging from the fuss they were
making, were evidently regarding me with terror.   It did not
take me long to find the first family—two young yellowbobs,

huddling against the roots of a tree, where their baby dress of brown merged into the surroundings, so that but for their cries they would have been passed unnoticed. The anxious "cheep, cheep" of their golden-breasted mother as she flew from tree to tree showed that she also was aware of my presence. I did not want to harrow their feelings unnecessarily, so I moved away to where a young fantail cuckoo sat huddled on a dead bush "peeking" fretfully, while two little brown tits worked fussily to feed him.

A little way further on a native canary passed me with food in his bill, and I watched him enter a sapling, where I knew there hung a cosy nest with two hungry chicks inside. But almost every bird I saw was either carrying food or looking for it, for little birds need their breakfasts just as much as any other children. Two razor-grinders flew hurriedly past to their nest high up in a tall gum, each with a morsel in its beak, a thrush went swiftly past, also carrying food to its nest in the hollow of a high tree. As I moved along towards the sandstone I heard a pathetic cry just above my head, and after some looking discovered two more baby Jacky Winters. They were younger than the one who had eaten his breakfast on my fence, but were already much too big for the tiny nest on which they huddled. It truly was "on" and not "in," for the little shallow nest soon ceases really to shelter the young birds. They saw me looking at them, and drew their heads back, trying to hide from sight. But, though they could no longer look at me, I could plainly see them as they bulged over the edges of their tiny home.

Down through the fence where the sandstone begins I had an experience very common in the mother months. I was walking quietly along, when suddenly, with an angry note, a bright olive bird flashed out from a bush beside me. It was the white-eared honey-eater, and I knew from the tone of her voice that she had babies close by. I stooped down to look for them, and immediately the bird flew almost against my face, and then to the ground a few yards ahead, fluttering along slowly, and dragging its wings painfully, as if they were broken. I advanced a step or two, but the bird for all her apparent helplessness always managed to keep ahead of me. On she fluttered, down the track, leading me further and further from her treasured darlings, then suddenly when she thought I was safely out of the way, with a cry she skimmed off into the bushes, and by a circular route went back to her babies.

It is a little trick to which most mother birds have recourse in the spring. The idea is that their apparent helplessness will tempt you to catch them, and so leave their babies unmolested. It is the natural mother instinct to protect its young at any cost; but unfortunately for the little birds, this very trick of the mother often attracts people's attention to their existence, instead of drawing them away. But I let the fond mother think she had deluded me, and went on my way. The cicadas were in full chorus by this time, floury bakers, double drummers, and the rest of them, and their song was almost deafening. But I managed to detect above their clamour the whispering note of the Lambert's blue wren—him with the chestnut shoulders on his blue and black coat. I stood patiently

Jacky Winter~*Microeca leucophaea*

for ten minutes before I was rewarded by the sight of him flying up with a tiny fly in his bill, which was welcomed by a chorus of squeaks from a grey spider-flower bush. There I saw three of the very quaintest of all young birds, three tiny brown balls, no bigger than half my thumb, and each with a tiny tail standing straight up in ridiculous imitation of its parent.

The last family of baby birds I found was right up on the sandstone heights, where, in a stunted banksia, lay three half-fledged babies of the tawny-crowned honey-eater. Three is an unusual number for a honey-eater's family, two being the regulation limit; but these three little brothers did not seem to mind being slightly crowded, and very happy they looked snuggling together in their cosy cradle, every now and then opening wide their yellow gapes at the prospect of a feed.

Although there are so many young abroad, numbers of the birds are still building, some for the second or third time this season. In the forest country the leaden flycatcher, which came south more than a month ago, has a beautiful cup-shaped nest, set in a dead branch of a tall tree. Another migratory bird, the reed-warbler, one of our sweetest singers, is also breeding, but I must go to the reed-beds to find it. In those same reed-beds will be found the wonderful little nest of the grass-warbler, an industrious little bird, which often covers its oval nest, made of fine grass, spiders' webs, and cocoons, with a big sheltering leaf stitched on with a silky substance in a marvellous manner. But the reed-beds are a long way from here, and I must return to my own district.

Here, the golden glory of the bush has departed, and now white is the reigning colour. One of the tea-trees is profusely in flower, covering whole paddocks; in its blossoms the beetles love to harbour, and they shine like enamel in the morning sun. Some gum-trees also add their white blossom to the harmony, and the creamy flowers of the dwarf apple are bursting out from their red woolly buds. Then, of course, there are the most prized of all white wild flowers, the flannel flowers, which just now are out in profusion, and are to be found in sandy soil amongst the rocks, which make a telling background for the white stars. Close by grow two other highly prized flowers, the Christmas bush, just now covered with its white blossoms, which in a week or so will give place to the red fruit, commonly mistaken for the flower; and the Christmas bells, most happily named of all our native flowers. These bells grow in the most unpromising places, and their gorgeous red and yellow show up brightly against the sandy background they love.

Another conspicuous blossom just now is the big hibbertia; its flower is very like a yellow dog-rose, and it is sometimes called the "sand-rose," because it grows so freely on the sand by the shore. But as a similar species grows just as freely in in brush, the name is not altogether appropriate.

In the sandstone country there are several smaller flowers in evidence; the most noticeable is the pink stylidium, or trigger plant as it is called, on account of its long style which springs back if touched. The three-petalled fringed violet also shows brightly, its warm purple making a charming contrast to the grey sandy background.

Christmas bells ~ *Blandfordia*

FLOWERS BLOOMING.

Hibbertia scandens	Yellow dog-rose
Hibbertia dentata	
Pultenaea villosa	Yellow pea-flower
Ceratopetalum gummiferum	Christmas bush
Angophora hispida	Dwarf apple
Melaleuca nodosa	} Tea-trees
Leptospermum flavescens	
Callistemon citrinus	Red bottlebrush
Actinotus helianthi	Flannel flower

Actinotus minor	Little flannel flower
Grevillea buxifolia	Grey spider-flower
Helichrysum diosmifolium	
Stylidium lineare	Trigger plant
Doryanthes excelsa	Gigantic lily
Blandfordia nobilis	} Christmas bells
Blandfordia grandiflora	
Thysanotus juncifolius	Fringed violet

BIRDS ARRIVING IN DECEMBER.

Apus pacificus	Fork-tailed Swift
Hirundapus caudacutus	Spine-tailed Swift
Glossopsitta concinna	Musk Lorikeet

BIRDS BREEDING IN DECEMBER.

Rhipidura fuliginosa	Grey Fantail
Rhipidura leucophrys	Willie Wagtail
Myiagra rubecula	Leaden Flycatcher
Malurus lamberti	Variegated Wren
Cisticola exilis	Golden-headed Cisticola
Acanthiza nana	Little Thornbill
Ephthianura albifrons	White-fronted Chat
Pachycephala rufiventris	Rufous-breasted Thickhead or Rufous Whistler
Lichenostomus chrysops	Yellow-faced Honeyeater
Aegintha temporalis	Red-browed Finch
Anthus novaeseelandiae	Richard's Pipit
Halcyon sanctus	Sacred Kingfisher
Cuculus variolosus	Brush Cuckoo
Coturnix australis	Brown Quail
Turnix varia	Painted Quail

JANUARY

Wild parsley ·
Lomatia silaifolia

D O you remember the story of the cicada who took the place of the broken note in the poet's lyre, and "saved the singer from defeat, with her chirrup low and sweet?"

It's a pretty story but could not have been told of an Australian cicada. He would never be satisfied to be merely one note of a song, nor even the whole song. He is content with nothing less than a full chorus, a cantata, an oratorio, or whatever is the singing that makes the most noise. He will brook no interference; he must have the whole stage to himself, and anything else that dares to interrupt is sung loudly down, while he goes through his summer performance. He has been in fine fettle during the past month—or perhaps I had better say they, for there are millions of him. They, then, have certainly taken possession of the bush during the past few weeks, and everything has had to give way before them. The bush tracks, and even the side paths of the high roads, are riddled with holes, out of which the creatures crept from their winter sleep a couple of months ago. The fences are scaly with the dry shells shed by them, while the gum trunks, especially the ironbarks, are spotted from head to foot with the same brown husks. On grey, damp days, I have found dozens of the newly-hatched—or should it be fledged?—cicadas clinging helplessly to posts and tree-trunks, waiting for their wings to dry. At such times they fall an easy prey to the ants, who devour them alive, and to their other enemy, the small boy. But though numbers perish in eaily youth, there are still left myriads upon myriads to swell the summer chorus, to drown the voices of the birds, and to tempt small boys to climb all sorts of impossible places in pursuit of them.

They have certainly done their best to make the past month what it has been, a noisy, noisy month. The bush has been robbed of much of its peacefulness since December came in; for, added to the deafening song of the cicada, and the shout of the boy in pursuit of him, there has been the invading army of flower-gatherers and picnickers, who have arrived in hordes, leaving desolation and many tins in their wake. They have dragged the maiden-hair up by its roots, torn the Christmas bushes to shreds, and plucked every Christmas bell for miles around. They have strewn their papers, tins, and fruit-peelings all over the sheltered spots and shady corners, and have thrown their broken bottles into the creeks and gullies. They have made the day hideous with their shrieks and noisy laughter, and the night a thing of pain with their camping songs.

But now the holidays are past, and the holiday-makers have returned to their daily round, leaving the cicadas in full possession. And, though they have scorned and insulted her, no doubt Nature has dropped a tiny gift upon each one of them, which, unconsciously, they will carry with them through the workaday world for many a day to come.

And now, just when the holiday-makers have left the bush to recover its accustomed peace, come still greater enemies— the hot wind and the bush fires. On every side the horizon is hidden in a cloud of smoke, and even the gum-leaves are drooping beneath the intense heat of the last few days. But though, when standing on the top of the hill, one sees nothing save a smoky haze, down in my own particular gully the only sign of the fire is the pungent smell which comes on the wind. It is far too hot through the daytime to venture out with any pleasure; but this evening, after sunset, I wended my way down into the cool of the gully. On the fence just at the bottom of the hill I saw four young wood-swallows, with mottled grey backs, sitting huddled together, evidently feeling the heat very badly, while a little further on a young rufous-breasted thickhead and his father sat gaping for breath in a tea-tree. Only a week ago I took my camera and photograph-ed that same little thickhead and his brother, then just out of their nest, and two more confiding little birds I never met. They let me catch them and stroke them without any trouble, and one sat comfortably on the back of my hand while I

walked about and fixed my camera.   I got a picture of the
two little chaps sitting side by side, calling to their father to
bring them something to eat.   But to-night only one little brother
was to be seen, and I am afraid that the other must have suc-
cumbed to the heat.

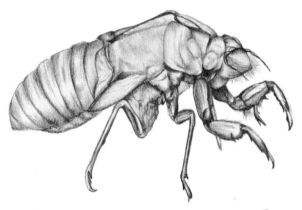

Cicada shell

Indeed, the whole bird world seemed to have been over-
come by the weather; there were very few to be seen, and those
that were about skulked silently in the shadow.   As I passed

down where the soakage from a garden on the hill creeps out, two peewees flew shrieking up from the moist spot, but even their noisy voices seemed less harsh than usual; and further down, amongst the white-blossomed bursaria bushes near the creek—now as dry as any road—a fan-tailed cuckoo wailed more fretfully than ever as two brown tits did their best to appease his hunger.

Although it is really more than midsummer, there are still a good many baby birds about. A week ago I saw a black-cap honey-eater feeding a pallid cuckoo, and the week before that I found a fantail's nest with young ones almost ready to fly. On the same day I found a kingfisher's nest with one pure white egg in a hole in a red gum, and in another week or so there will be the squawking of baby kingfishers coming from that tree. Last Saturday, when walking over the heath towards the sea, I came upon three of the sweetest of all baby birds, three little chats, or chitwees, as the boys call them, which had just left their cup-shaped nest in a low thick bush.

The red gums just now are things of beauty, with their dry bark dropping off in great pieces, leaving the soft flesh pink of the new skin below. This evening, as I walked amongst them, their trunks were flushed from palest pink to deep blood-red in the fierce sunset glow, making a magic wood of my peaceful valley. Amongst the rocks, where the creek ran three months ago, I found two snow-white bushes gleaming in the twilight; they were blueberry ashes (Elaeocarpus cyaneus), which later

on will be covered with dark-blue berries.   There is not a
more ornamental tree in the bush than this, with its glossy

leaves and wealth of white blossoms, which very much resemble
the garden deutzia, and it is a wonder it is not more cultivated

by gardeners. How the bushes came to be left undisturbed by the picnickers is a wonder, unless they were too busy tearing to pieces the Christmas bushes, mutilated remains of which marked the vandal's progress all the way.

Although it was late when I reached the spot where the creek should join the main stream, it was not too dark to see the rosy flush of a tall coachwood in full blossom. The coachwood is first cousin to the Christmas bush and though its leaves are bigger its calyx is just as red and effective as that of the better-known species. Evidently the picnickers hadn't penetrated so far down the gully, as the tree was absolutely untouched, and stood in perfect beauty in the evening light. Near by, the tall flower spikes of the wild parsley gleamed white in the gloaming. This flower, orchid-like in its creamy beauty, is out in profusion just now, and is one of the few blossoms in evidence on the sandstone that has been robbed of its Christmas bells.

The daylight had faded into moonlight as I turned for home. The moon, red through the smoke haze, wrapped the bush path in mystic shadows, which seemed to hide all sorts of wondrous secrets. In the distance a boobook owl called softly; from the bushes close by came the stirrings and sleepy chirpings of tired birds. A little cool whisper of a breeze ran down the gully to tell of the approaching southerly; and when I reached the top of the hill, the clump of tall apple-trees (Angophora intermedia) that crowns the summit was waving blossom-laden branches in the grateful breeze which had arrived from the south.

Kingfisher

These apples, which most people mistake for gum-trees, are the most noticeable flowers in the bush this month; and in many places whole paddocks are white with them, as they stretch their graceful branches over the white shrubs of the flowering box just breaking out into blossom.

FLOWERS BLOOMING.

Bursaria spinosa	White box or blackthorn
Brachychiton acerifolium	
Elaeocarpus reticulatus	Blueberry ash
Ceratopetalum gummiferum	Christmas bush
Ceratopetalum apetalum	Coachwood
Angophora floribunda	Apple tree
Lomatia silaifolia	Wild parsley
Blandfordia nobilis	Christmas bell
Thysanotus juncifolius	Fringed violet
Dipodium punctatum	Native hyacinth

BIRDS BREEDING IN JANUARY.

Rhipidura fuliginosa	Grey Fantail
Ephthianura albifrons	White-fronted Chat
Cisticola exilis	Golden-headed Cisticola
Pachycephala rufiventris	Yellow-faced Honeyeater
Phylidonyris novaehollandiae	New Holland Honeyeater
Zosterops lateralis	Silvereye
Dicaeum hirundinaceum	Mistletoe-bird
Halcyon sanctus	Sacred Kingfisher
Coturnix australis	Brown Quail
Turnix varia	Painted Quail

FEBRUARY

O^N SATURDAY we took our breakfast out. The bush is always sweet and fresh at 6 o'clock in the morning, even though the spell of dry weather has scorched and withered the last remaining signs of spring's fairness. The glade, which awhile ago was green and grassy, is now brown and parched, but the dry grass makes a comfortable seat, and in the creek bed, which has been guiltless of water these three months past, we found a cosy resting place and a good spot for our fire. A breakfast of hard-boiled eggs, fresh pears, and muscatel grapes is a feast for the gods when eaten beneath the shade of turpentines, with the blue smoke curling up from the little fire where the billy boils; and we sat in lazy contentment, dawdling over our meal and watching a Jacky Winter in chase of his. Quietly he sits on a branch, his bright eyes watching all around for his prey. A little moth comes fluttering by. Jacky skims the air towards him, the moth dodges, but the bird is too quick, and a click of the mandibles tells us that so much breakfast is safely caught. Then he flies back to his branch to eat at his leisure and watch for the next course.

Then a yellowbob came to visit us, and perched on the side of a tree trunk, watched us with big friendly eyes. He is always very inquisitive about picnics, and comes to investigate whenever he sees a cloth laid on the grass. There is no bird

in the bush more friendly
than he, and in a little while
he was hopping round us
picking up the crumbs gently
scattered for his benefit.

Suddenly from the clump
of tea-trees behind us came
a whirring noise, and a large
light bird flew rapidly by to
the fence across the green,
where he perched clumsily
with an upward flick of his
tail. It was a young pallid
cuckoo in his transition
dress of speckled brown and
white, which looks rather
as if he had been liberally
splashed with the white-wash
brush. He was probably the
same chap we had seen last
month being fed by chickups,

but though we watched for some time we saw no sign of the
foster parents. Although the pallid cuckoos have been silent
now for some weeks past they have not yet gone off on their
northward flight, and no doubt the parents of this young fellow
were somewhere near, ready to call him when the time came

for departure.   There were no other birds about the glade, which is generally so gay with songs and flutterings.   The dry weather has driven them all further down the creek bed, where they can still find a little water.   So when we had idled to our heart's content over our tea and fruit we hid our basket beneath the white-flowered bursaria bushes and started off down the gully.

Such a quiet gully it was.   One could hardly believe it was the same place that three months ago blazed and glowed in all its spring gorgeousness.   But, though the gay splendour had departed, there was plenty to watch and wonder at, for there is never a month in the year when the marvels of the bush

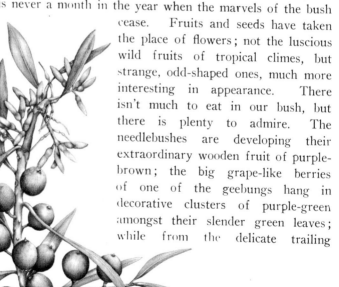

cease.   Fruits and seeds have taken the place of flowers; not the luscious wild fruits of tropical climes, but strange, odd-shaped ones, much more interesting in appearance.   There isn't much to eat in our bush, but there is plenty to admire.   The needlebushes are developing their extraordinary wooden fruit of purple-brown; the big grape-like berries of one of the geebungs hang in decorative clusters of purple-green amongst their slender green leaves; while from the delicate trailing

Geebung ~ *Persoonia*

Banksia cone

greenery of the eustrephus hang the small yellow balls which give it its name, blackfellow's orange. The blueberry ash, which two months ago was white with blossom, is now covered with berries already ripening to the required colour.

There are still a few flowers in bloom. The white thorn, or bursaria, is the most noticeable thing in the bush, as it will be for the next few months, and its tiny blossoms hold a nutty fragrance that makes it a very acceptable flower for the house —if you don't mind the thorns—in this season of scarcity. Then there is one of the geebungs in flower, too, with deep yellow spikes of bloom amongst its bright green needle leaves. Wild parsley, too, rears its creamy white flower heads amongst the green, but except for these, and a pale wattle, and a small mauve weed (Eranthemum) which grows all along the roadsides, blossoming time is done.

For it is the time of maturity. Seeds and fruit have taken the place of flowers; young trees have put off their infant leaves of red and copper, and have donned their grown-up gowns of green; while the trunks of the older trees have shed their last year's sheaths, and emerged in splendid garments of purest cream, or mottled greys and reds and blues.

The birds, too, have passed the baby age. No longer comes the sweet twittering of mother-talk and baby answerings. The families have long since left their nests, and are travelling round together. Their education is in full swing; the parent birds do not now carry flies and grubs to hungry waiting mouths, for the chicks are all hunting for themselves. But they are still in family groups; and though the young ones can use their wings and catch their dinners, the big world is full of unknown dangers, and they fly back to their parents at the first sound of alarm. Half-way down the gully we met a family of yellow-bobs, the two youngsters distinguishable from their parents by the streaks of brown still discernible on the coats of green, grey and yellow. A family of thrushes played about in the tree tops, the glad voices of the parents ringing out every now and then in encouragement.

It is really a month of *debutantes,* for all the young birds are entering into the arena of life, and are trying their little voices in the universal song. At present they are all garbed in their distinctive gowns, which, by-and-by, they will change for the more conspicuous livery of grown-ups. By this time next year they will all be bringing out sons and daughters of their own, but now youth and freedom are theirs.

Altogether it is a fascinating time in the bush, this time of transition and fulfilment. And already on some of the early wattles are to be seen the tiniest of tiny buds, which tell of the flowers to come, and of the eternal cycle which never ceases.

FLOWERS BLOOMING.

Bursaria spinosa	White box, blackthorn
Acacia longissima	Fine-leafed wattle
Lomatia silaifolia	Wild parsley
Persoonia pinifolia	
Pseuderanthemum variabile	

FRUIT.

Elaeocarpus reticulatur	Blueberry ash
Hakea sericea	
Hakea teretifolia	
Persoonia hirsuta	Geebungs
Eustrephus latifolius	Blackfellow's oranges

BIRDS DEPARTING IN FEBRUARY.

Myiagra rubecula	Leaden Flycatcher
Myzomela sanguinolenta	Scarlet Honeyeater
Cuculus pallidus	Pallid Cuckoo
Cuculus variolosus	Square-tailed or Brush Cuckoo

BIRDS BREEDING IN FEBRUARY.

Dicaeum hirundinaceum	Mistletoe-bird
Coturnix australis	Brown Quail
Turnix varia	Painted Quail

Eastern Yellow Robin - Eopsaltria australis

MARCH

I T HAS been a wonderful February. Instead of four weeks of steaming muggy days and stifling nights, we have had long breaks of cool, fresh days, and nights when a blanket was a comfort, with just a few odd days here and there to remind us of what a Sydney February really can be.

And yesterday the last day of the month broke in a thick white mist that shrouded the world in a winter pall. Quite cold and shivery it was, too, and altogether more like May or June than the second month of the year.

It was a very fascinating morning for a walk, and by seven o'clock we had had a cup of tea, donned our coats and thickest boots, and were on our way down the gully. Of all the beautiful bush times there are, I know of none more delicious than an early misty morning, when the mist is not cold and dank, but soft and cool, as it was this morning. It rests on your cheek like a fairy down, damps your hair into curl, cools and freshens your whole body, and sends you swinging along your path with head erect, sniffing the fresh earth smells all round you.

Stenocarpus sinuatus

We were not the only ones in the gully; down in the clearing, now vividly green, we came across a little family party, father, mother, and three children, all busily employed picking mushrooms. A full basket was the reward of their labour, and they told us there were more farther on across the paddock. But though mushrooms have a charm of their own not to be denied, their fascination was not strong enough to draw us from the path which leads down by the fence, through the sliprails, into the part where the tall blackbutts grow. Up in their high tops two butcher birds were calling to each other, the rich contralto notes of the first bird answered in rippling mezzo by his mate. The butcher birds are free from the housekeeping cares which kept them down in the valleys during the summer, and have come back to the ridge for the winter; and now every morning is made musical by their ringing voices. Most of the birds have finished with family cares for the season, and with the young ones launched on their ways, the parent birds are taking it easy, and sing with a freer, surer tone than has been heard since the nesting commenced. The path beneath the blackbutts led us through into the rocky scrub where the stunted apples and banksias grow in a thickly-matted mass. The apple trees are covered with their fascinating fruit; the creamy blossom has vanished, and in its place are those quaint brown seed-pods with their little caps, now vividly red, which in a week or so will split up into three sections and let the little seeds out. The banksias, too, are very attractive at present, with their new cones forming; they look such soft, velvety things, these embryo bottle brushes, but are really quite hard and knobby to the touch. The white-cheeked honey-eaters love this patch of apple and banksia; dozens of them were darting about, playing chasings through the bushes and calling to each other as they flew, "You saucy girl, you saucy girl." Spiders seem to love this patch, too, and every few yards we had to step aside to avoid breaking down a beautiful dew-bespangled web. The mist was clearing now, and the sunshine falling through the trees touched the spider-webs into a mesh of gleaming pearls, in the midst of which the spider lurked in his den, a curled-up leaf.

Welcome Swallow - *Hirundo neoxena*

It showed us something else more interesting than the spider's web. In a big grey gum at the edge of the track to the gully, we saw one of Nature's most marvellous devices for protecting her creatures. Jutting out from the main trunk was what appeared to be a broken limb, but a closer glance

Brown Quail - *Coturnix australis*

showed that it was a bird, or rather two birds. Cuddling very close together were two frog-mouths, or moreporks, sitting bolt upright like stiff pieces of wood, the striped grey of their coats barely distinguishable from the bark of the tree. A hundred people would have passed right by without seeing them, but the bush lover's eye is quick to detect, and we enjoyed the quaint sight before us. These birds, by the way, do not utter the "more-pork" sound popularly ascribed to them, but which really belongs to the boobook owl; their note is a soft "Oom, oom, oom."

Further on, where the slope drops down to the creek, we roused a family of quail. The little ones, half-grown, scuttled quickly to cover, and immediately became invisible, but the parents kept on ahead of us, running with lifted heads and a funny tip-toe effect. We followed them for some yards, keeping them easily in sight; then, when they thought we were safely out of reach of their chicks, they disappeared in the bushes and doubled back.

There were very few flowers to be seen; a stray blossom of pultenaea, or grevillea, remained here and there to tell of vanished glory, but the only plants really in full flower were a pale creamy wattle and a tea-tree, which raised long spikes of blossom from its dull green leaves. The wattle was drenched with dew, but a slight shake sent the drops scattering, and shed a nutty sweetness on the air.

It is the resting time in the bush; the time when birds and flowers and insects, having all produced their share of life and beauty, rest for a while before beginning once again the joyful task allotted them by Mother Nature.

FLOWERS BLOOMING.

Acacia longissima   Fine-leafed wattle
Leptospermum scoparium   Tea-tree
Stenocarpus sinuatus   Wheel flower
Lobelia gracilis

BIRDS DEPARTING IN MARCH.

Lalage sueurii   White-winged Triller
Gerygone olivacea   Native Canary or White-throated
                              Warbler
Pachycephala rufiventris   Rufous-breasted Thickhead or
                              Rufous Whistler
Hirundo neoxena   Welcome Swallow
Apus pacificus   Fork-tailed Swift
Hirundapus caudacutus   Spine-tailed Swift
Halcyon sanctus   Sacred Cuckoo

BIRDS BREEDING IN MARCH.

Phylidonyris novaehollandiae   New Holland Honeyeater
Phylidonyris nigra   White-cheeked Honeyeater
Phylidonyris melanops   Tawny-crowned Honeyeater
Coturnix australis   Brown Quail

Grevillea

APRIL

A T SIX o'clock this morning the sky was pink from rim to rim with rosy clouds, that sent their glow on to the tips of the tree-tops and wakened all the birds of the neighbourhood into song. Not that there are very many birds about just now, for the northward flight has been in progress for several weeks past, and many of the birds have gone to warmer climes for the winter months. The cuckoos have all left the neighbourhood, and we miss the ringing notes of the pallid and the brush cuckoos, and the melancholy wail of the bronze. The native canaries, too, have departed northwards, and their running song no longer makes music amongst the saplings in the gully. Quite at the beginning of the month the blood-birds (red-headed honey-eater) had taken their flight, and their gleaming red and black shine no longer amongst the gum-tips.

But although so many birds have gone, there are still enough left to greet the dawn with a chorus of song. The Jacky Winters are gaining in vigour as the cool days approach, for their song is always at its fullest and sweetest in the winter; the blue wrens, with their families, join in united efforts to swell the chorus; thrushes send their ringing notes across from tree to tree; razor-grinders utter their sweet, soft note, so different to the whirring, grinding one which gives them their name; and the kookaburras are most insistent of all in their rejoicing that the cool days are coming.

It was the kookaburras that woke me this morning. A family of them has been brought up down in the gully, and now that the youngsters are able to travel round with their parents the whole f a m i l y c o m e s u p e v e r y dawn-tide and greets the sun from a tall gum-tree just outside my garden fence. There they give loud expression to their enjoyment of life; the old ones are glad that their family is safely reared, and the young ones are glad they are alive, and so they lift their voices, and laugh and laugh at the whole world. This morning I felt that they were laughing at me for being such a lie-a-bed, when the sky was all rosy-flushed and the world was so sweet. It was ludicrous. Even though from my verandah bed I can see

Kookaburra - *Dacelo novaeguineae*

away over tree-tops and paddocks to the mountains, it is not the same as being out in the morning.   I don't like to be laughed at, even by kookaburras, who laugh at everyone and everything, so I jumped out of bed, and in less than half an hour was on my way down to the bush.

I might as well confess that it was not only the kookaburras and the charm of the morning that allured me out.   I wanted to find some flowers to fill my vases, for my garden is very bare at present, and I have to depend almost entirely on the spoils of the bush.   There are no flowers now in the gully, and I knew that I should have to go on to the sandstone before I should find any.   Just where the two types of country meet and merge I came to a regular wattle grove; not the golden wattle of the poets, but a soft, creamy sort which has a beauty of its own.   There were two kinds growing together and a few weeks back they were in full beauty; but now they are nearly over, and the ground beneath was strewn with the creamy powder of their flowers.   But I found two other wattles a little further on, which were in full bloom—the juniper-leafed wattle, with its pale gold balls, which was too prickly to pick; and the Port Jackson wattle, with its leaflets dark above and pale below, of which I picked a bunch.

Pushing on towards the river, I came across a perfect bower of blossoms.   Amongst the big grey rocks and beneath the scraggly, scribbly gums there grew a thick mass of the daintiest white blossom; its umbels of tiny white flowers swayed on the end of slender stems, and the light soft breeze turned all towards me. It was the wild parsnip, one of the freest autumn flowerers. In bright contrast to its fragile paleness, the deep pink stars of the crowea shone amongst the grey rocks—its favourite habitat. It has not yet reached its zenith, and the unfolded buds lend a warm note of colour to the scene. Beyond the rocks, but still in the picture, was a thick clump of tea-tree covered with long flower-spikes of pink and white blossom. Some of the bushes had nearly finished blooming, and the bright red of their seeds made vivid contrast. It was a corner that, in its delicacy of colouring, suggested spring rather than autumn; but the supreme disregard for the seasons is one of the chief charms of our bush flowers. Spring, summer, autumn, or winter, there are always some of them making the land lovely with their sweetness and colour.

In a very short time I had my arms as full as they would hold. At least, I thought so, until I caught sight, just ahead, of a tall banksia, covered with gorgeous flower-spikes, their rich bronze-red glowing in the morning light. It was Banksia ericifolia, one of the handsomest of the honeysuckles, or bottle brushes as they are alternately called. There is, I think, no more decorative plant in the bush than this particular banksia. when the bottlebrushes are newly-opened and the little hooked styles are deep red with yellow tips. A bunch of them arranged with their own green in a big bronze jar is a sight to gladden a whole household, and whether they have the plain green paper of my study or the brown of my hall for background, they are always a much-to-be-desired decoration. So, laying the other blossoms down in a cool spot, I was soon stretching on tip-toe to pick the coveted beauties.

As I was pushing through some thick undergrowth to reach a specially fine one, a bird flew out past my face with a frightened, scolding note. It was a New Holland honey-eater, of which there were, as usual, a number about. From the tone of his note I suspected a nest, and after a few minutes' search came upon the little cradle, set low in another banksia, with two half-fledged baby birds cuddling together at the bottom. The New Holland and the white-cheeked honey-eaters both have a distinct autumn breeding season, and as the scrubby banksia country is their favourite nesting place, I looked about for more nests. After half an hour's search I was rewarded by finding another New Holland's with one egg, and a half-finished nest; also two white-cheeked honey-eaters', one with two creamy-pink eggs and one with two bare little nestlings.

Crowea saligna

On my way home I came across one of the little tragedies of nature. I was crossing a cleared space, and on the grass ahead of me saw a bird fluttering along in a peculiar way. I recognised it at once as a Jacky Winter, but I had never seen one flying in that manner. As I drew nearer I saw the reason why. The poor little thing had a wounded wing. I stooped to pick him up to examine it closer, when immediately an angry parent flew down from a tree and, scolding loudly, brushed quite close to my face, while her mate chattered furiously from the tree. I caught the little sufferer, which fluttered violently for a few minutes, then subsided into frightened quietness. I saw at once what had happened. The shot from a catapult had wounded the shoulder joint, but the wing was not broken, though it was stiff with blood and needed relaxing. I decided to carry the little bird home and doctor it. My flowers, which I had laid on the ground, were as much as my hands would hold, but I have a side pocket in my bush skirt with a flap which buttons over. Into this I carefully put the Jacky, who nestled down with a frightened little peek; then I went on my way pursued by the angry anxious notes of the parents.

A little warm water and boracic worked wonders with the wounded wing, and after keeping the little bird all day in an empty cage (to which he seemed to grow almost reconciled after a time, especially when I brought him some little white grubs), I carried him back to the clearing and let him loose. He was immediately greeted by his parents, who flew round and round in wild excitement. After a few timid ineffectual efforts the young bird managed to flutter up into a sapling, where I left him, feeling that there was no longer any cause for fear of his safety, and that by the morning he would be well enough to fly out of range of the marauding small boys and their catapults.

FLOWERS BLOOMING.

Crowea saligna	
Acacia longissima	Fine-leafed wattle
Acacia linifolia	
Acacia terminalis	Port Jackson wattle
Acacia ulicifolia	Juniper-leafed wattle
Leptospermum scoparium	Tea-tree
Platysace ericoides	Wild parsnip
Grevillea speciosa	Red spider-flower
Grevillea buxifolia	Grey spider-flower
Banksia ericifolia	Honeysuckle, or bottlebrush
Lambertia formosa	Honey flower
Lobelia gracilis	
Commelina cyanea	Wandering jew

BIRDS ARRIVING IN APRIL.

Anthochaera carunculata   Red Wattlebird

BIRDS DEPARTING IN APRIL.

Glossopsitta concinna   Musk Lorikeet

BIRDS BREEDING IN APRIL.

Phylidonyris novaehollandiae	New Holland Honeyeater
Phylidonyris nigra	White-cheeked Honeyeater
Aegintha temporalis	Red-browed Finch

MAY

THERE are some days that make you laugh; days when little white clouds chase each other across a smiling sky, when little breezes play round the tree-tops and tickle the leaves into laughter; when wavelets skip and dance in the harbour, and birds gush and gurgle in the bush; when the whole world laughs with joy and you must laugh with it.

To-day was just such a magic day; it came in with a frolicking breeze, and was welcomed by a burst of bird laughter. Blue wrens hopped cheerily across my grass plot; chickups called with throaty happy notes from the saplings. Jacky Winters were insistent on the fact that it was "sweeter, sweeter, sweeter;" and down in the valley the voice of the thrush

Five-corners ~ *Styphelia longifolia*

rang out with a happy peal. Everything was calling—
"Come and play; come and be happy;" and when the
whole world calls like that, who am I to stay at home and
work?

It was a day made for joy, and for the bush. There were
many things I might have done in town. There was the pro-
cession, there was the "Commem.," there were football matches,
and matinees, and a dozen other things that are counted pleasure.
But, on the other hand, there was the bush, with its thousand
joys, calling with insistent voice—and the bush won.

The calendar tells us that May is the first of the winter
months, and according to all traditions the bush should now be
bare and silent. There is not certainly the wild luxuriance of
spring and summer, but the bush is far from bare; the Port
Jackson wattle is in full bloom, and its pale cream balls and
glossy green leaves are just as beautiful in their way as the
more striking blooms of the golden spring flowers. Amongst
the rocks down near the river this wattle grows in great soft
masses against a background of sassafras and turpentine; out on
the coast it grows less luxuriantly, but everywhere about Sydney
it is to be seen—and smelt, for it is very sweet. There are two
other pale wattles going off now, but here and there a branch of
blossom remains to bear witness to the fact that wattles do not
all belong to spring.

The grey rocks in the gully, which give such pleasure to

the eye in the hot dry summer months, would look very dour and cold just now were it not for the glowing pink blossoms of the crowea, which cast a cheerful gleam through the shadows, and catch on their round pink faces the glinting sunbeams that come dancing down through the leaves. For the spirit of laughter has followed me down into the valley, and even the grey rocks smile as the shadows of the leaves flicker playfully over them. Higher up the bank a host of red spider-flowers jig like living things to the music of the wind. The grevilleas are splendid winter bloomers; and the red one is particularly profuse just now, and very gay is the note of colour it lends to the landscape.

But sweet though it was down in the valley, it was a day for high places and sunshine. I crossed the creek, now quite dry, and climbed up the other side. Here I found a clump of joyful colour, where the brown and yellow pea-blossoms of the bossiaea looked like butterflies dancing on their quaint flat stems. Close by the last blue flowers of the lobelia swayed brightly in the breeze, looking each moment as if the slender stems must snap and let the flowers dance off. As I climbed higher I found a few stray blossoms of the red epacris, which seems to flower all the year round, and when I reached the uplands once again, I was greeted with the sight of the "five-corner" with pale green blossoms opening to the sun.

It was while I was looking at the quaint tubular blossoms of my childhood's friend that I heard a familiar note that also

seemed to belong to long ago.
"Sck, sck," it went, and in a
moment by flew a redhead,
or, as serious people would
call him, a red-eyebrowed
finch.   But it wasn't at all a
serious day, so I called him
redhead, and followed him
softly through the bushes.
He did not take much
notice of me, but flew on
to a thick needlebush, where
high amongst the prickly
leaves I saw the familiar
long, retort-shaped nest.   As
he approached I could hear a
very faint squeaking, and
knew that at the end of that
long nest some little bird-
lings were waiting hungrily
for the seed which the father
was bringing.

I went on my way with a
song at my heart, glad that I
had met this little friend of
my childhood on this playing
day.

And never was there such a day for playing. According to all traditions winter should be sad and silent, and there should be no birds with happy song. But this dear, contrary land of ours loves to upset traditions, and instead of flying off to summer quarters, or skulking in the bushes, lots of birds are trilling forth their sweetest songs. There are very few now burdened with domestic cares. The white-cheeked and New Holland honey-eaters still have eggs and young ones to look after, and a few belated redheads are bringing out their families; but the majority of birds are free to enjoy life, and though many have migrated, there is a chorus of full bird voices such as has not been heard since the early spring. All through the summer we heard nothing but baby talk; now the parents are singing in their normal voices, and the young birds now well grown, are also trying theirs. And if the chorus is not as complete as in the springtide, there is nothing sad and melancholy about those bird notes that ring through bush and gully, and tell the world that though summer is over and winter is here, there is still plenty of sunshine and joy in this beautiful land of ours.

FLOWERS BLOOMING.

Crowea saligna	
Pimelea linifolia	
Bossiaea heterophylla	Yellow pea-flower
Acacia terminalis	Port Jackson wattle
Acacia longissima	Fine-leafed wattle
Acacia linifolia	
Acacia ulicifolia	Juniper-leafed wattle

Acacia suaveolens	Sweet-scented wattle
Callistemon citrinus	Bottlebrush
Platysace lanceolata	
Grevillea speciosa	Red spider-flower
Grevillea sericea	
Hakea sericea	
Styphelia longifolia	
Styphelia tubiflora	Five-corners
Styphelia laeta	
Leucopogon microphyllus	Whitebeard
Wahlenbergia gracilis	Blue bell
Lobelia gracilis	
Lobelia dentata	
Pseuderanthemum variabile	

BIRDS BREEDING IN MAY.

Menura novaeseelandiae   Superb Lyrebird

fledgling birds

JUNE

IT IS too wet now to go out in the very early morning, for this is the season of heavy dews and soft white mists. Every morning the valley is filled with white clouds, which mark the river bed and sometimes hide the hills as well. The grass and trees are drenched almost till noon, and even in the middle of the morning if I venture down my gully to gather ferns I feel like the young man in the "Elegy"—

Brushing with hasty steps the dews away.

There is a great charm in feeling like a person in a poem, and there is a distinct joy in wading through dew-wet grass and shaking down the drops from the laden branches; but for a good, comfortable bush walk the afternoon is the best time just now.

So as early as possible after lunch I set out. I turned my back on the gully, where now there is nothing to be found but maiden-hair, crossed the railway line, and struck out to the east. There was a warmth in the air; not the decadent warmth of an unseasonable autumn day, but a gentle, caressing glow that was almost a foretaste of spring. Perhaps it was the

wattles coming into bloom in the gardens along the road which
completed the illusion, but certainly I had a distinct spring feeling in my blood, and I meant to see if there was any sign of spring
in the bush.

My last bush walk had been almost a sad one, everything
was so dry; but the rain had come since then, and after it the
heavy dews, and I felt justified in expecting to see some flowers.
It was pleasant after my last crackly tramp to feel the leaves
soft and moist underfoot, so I chose the deepest and dampest
gully I could find.   As I picked my way along the rocky path
that could scarcely be called a track, pink crowea glowed on all
sides, and, though I knew crowea to be truly a winter flower,
my hopes of spring blooms ran high.   And I had not hoped
in vain; for out of the sheltered tangle, still dripping with the
morning dew, peeped many shy flowers, not yet in their full
spring splendour, but giving promise of the glory to come.   Bush
things do not seem to fully recognise the existence of a winter
season.   On the bleak hill-tops they may be suppressed, but give
them a little shelter and a little moisture and they will always do
their best to make June look like August.

Three wattles in three different stages showed up boldly
against the green background of the creek bed. The slender-
leaved wattle was nearly over, only a few pale blossoms remaining, but the Port Jackson wattle was still in full swing.
Many of its balls of yellow floss had been matted together by
the rain, but fresh clusters of a deeper gold told a tale of

happier times. On a little flat by the creek the sweet-scented wattle had burst into bloom, and as I gathered its fragrant spikes I rolled its name round my tongue. "Suaveolens," the men of science call it, and for once they have found a happy name. The word shapes itself softly and sweetly from the lips, just as the flower breaks gently and deliciously from its full round bud. Other wattles may show more riotous masses of colour, but none is so sweet as this gentle plant, rearing a slender grey stem above the undergrowth to bear a modest head of creamy blossom, which delicately scents each passing breeze.

Tetratheca ericifolia

Underfoot the deep pink four-petalled flower of tetratheca lent a touch of colour to the grass, and with it grew the little flannel flower, which seems to bloom throughout the year; here and there its larger cousin put out a sickly bloom, miserably unlike its summer crop. The green-flowered five-corner was in full bloom, and the red-blossomed species was everywhere among the rocks. This last is an unsatisfactory little flower; though its blossoms are a charming colour, they always look as if they were just going off. But the spinebills seemed perfectly satisfied with them, for they darted among them everywhere with sharp, clapping wings, dipping their slender bills deep into the tubular blossoms.

Another quaint flower I found among the rocks was chloanthes; it has no other name. Its crinkly leaves give it a mossy look, and form a soft, subdued background for the queer little pale green, bell-shaped flowers. As I stooped to pick it a glimpse of pale mauve caught my eye, and I gasped with astonishment. An orchid, a caladenia—surely here was the spring I was seeking! But on making towards it I found it was no orchid, but only a washed-out snake-flower, which fell from its stalk at my touch. "Scaevola hispida" is the name botanists give it, but we always knew it as snake-flower when we were children, and there was a tradition amongst us that to eat the blossom was a certain antidote to snakebite.

Leaving the tangle of undergrowth behind me I passed on and came out on the brink of a rocky precipice which over-looked the junction of two deep gorges; down beyond gleamed the blue waters of Middle Harbour; round about me grew thickly a tall needlebush, covered with tiny cream blossoms; it is the needlebush which has the smallest of flowers, yet its seeds are about the largest. Tangled in amongst the needle-bush, and spreading out over the rocks, the white shafts of the heath-like lysinema climbed to a prodigious height, some spikes being three to four feet tall. It was a lovely picture, the grey rocks and pale flowers, lit by the afternoon sun, and

I stretched myself full length on the rock, humming the line :—
> What is so rare as a day in June?

The answer came back very quickly from a butcher-bird, that sent his song up from the valley below; his ringing notes were immediately answered by his mate from the other side of the gully, and I lay and listened with delight to the sweet duet. It was a duet with an occasional chorus, in which thrushes, yellowbobs, spinebills, and chickups all joined at intervals. Even the little rock-warblers joined their chirrup to the choir, as they hopped about the rocks, coming quite close to me as I lay silently listening.

But suddenly the chorus was disturbed by a more powerful note, which came round and ringing from the valley. I sat up quickly; there was no mistaking that note—it was the lyre-bird's. Then in a flash I remembered again that it was June, and that June is the time when the lyre-bird breeds. Supposing I should find the nest? I knew the bird built somewhere in these gullies; time and again I had heard their voices as they mimicked the other birds of the bush, and so wild was the country all about that it was more like a far-off mountain scene than the outskirts of the city. It was a typical spot for the lyre-bird's nest. Why shouldn't I look for it? And why shouldn't I find it? June is always my lucky month, and why should it fail me now?

I wasted no more time in conjectures, but jumped up, and walked along the rocks at the edge. I had not gone more

than a dozen yards when suddenly, almost below me, a large
brown bird shot out from the ground, and skimmed down the
gorge, with rounded wings. It was a hen lyre-bird. Almost
beside myself with excitement, I scrambled down, and there,
at the foot of a big blue gum, on a jutting rock, with a com-
manding view, was the nest I had so often longed to see. A
large, loosely-made nest it was, formed of sticks, and lined with
bark and moss and roots and feathers; through the large entrance at the side I could see quite plainly into it, and there in
the hollow lay one beautiful purple-tinged grey egg. Very carefully I put my hand in, and lifted it out, to gaze at the spots
and blotches which beautified its surface; and very proud of
myself I felt as I looked.

For the lyre-bird's nest is one of the hardest of all to find,
so safely is it hidden away as a rule in mountain fastnesses.
Yet here was I, half a dozen miles from the General Post
Office, holding this much-coveted treasure in my hand. And
I laughed to myself as I thought how egg-collectors would
envy me this find. Very gently I put the egg back in its
hiding place, and after making mental notes of the exact
position, turned homewards. In a month or so I will go back
and find a fluffy chick perhaps, but in the meantime the egg
must be left in secret safety.

Do you wonder why I sang as I went back through the
bush? I had come out to look for springtime in June, and
had found flowers and birds, and greatest treasure of all, the
lyre-bird's home.

FLOWERS BLOOMING.

Tetratheca ericifolia	
Crowea saligna	
Bossiaea heterophylla	} Yellow pea-flowers
Bossiaea scolopendria	
Acacia suaveolens	Sweet-scented wattle
Acacia longissima	Fine-leafed wattle
Acacia terminalis	Port Jackson wattle
Acacia linifolia	
Platysace ericoides	Wild parsnip
Platysace linearifolia	
Actinotus minor	Little flannel flower
Hakea propinqua	
Hakea sericea	Needlebush
Persoonia linearis	
Chloanthes stoechadis	
Styphelia tubiflora	} Five-corners
Styphelia longifolia	
Leucopogon microphyllus	Whitebeard
Epacris pulchella	
Woollsia pungens	White heath
Monotoca elliptica	

BIRDS BREEDING IN JUNE.

Acanthiza chrysorrhoa	Tomtit or Yellow-rumped Thornbill
Phylidonyris novaehollandiae	New Holland Honeyeater
Menura novaeseelandiae	Superb Lyrebird

Dragonfly

JULY

ALREADY "the hounds of spring are on winter's traces." Although it is only the first week of July, the resting time is over, and millions upon millions of little buds are just waiting the signal to burst into flower. In the suburbs the gardens are gorgeous with the golden splendour of the Queensland wattle, which is out in its full glory, and the moonlit air at night is heavy with its fragrance. The Cootamundra wattle is also coming on well, and another week or so will find it out-rivalling the northern beauty. As you walk along the high-road your eye is caught on every side by great heaps of gold massed against the blue sky, and the ear catches the drone of myriads of bees feeding amongst the blossoms.

But, fascinating though a walk along the high-road is this crisp cold weather, the bush is still more alluring. The days of rain have washed and sweetened the whole world, the soft drops have coaxed the buds to open just enough to let loose

Sprengelia
incarnata

some of their sweetness, and the smell of spring is everywhere. To-day as I walked along the sandy track on the top of the ridge, every sense responded to the fascinations of the season, and my eyes and ears and nose were all keenly aware of the delights around me.   Almost before I had passed the last houses on the road I was greeted by the nutty fragrance of the sweet-scented wattle, and my eyes were prepared for the masses of soft cream blossom which shone through the bushes on every side.   This wattle, which is truly a winter flower, is at its very best just now, and most of its crumpled buds have unfolded. But close by I found another wattle which has not yet passed the fascinating stage; the small bushes of the myrtle-leafed wattle are warmly red with their richly-coloured stalks and red-tinged buds.   It is not one of the most conspicuous bloomers, but in its early stage it has a charm of its own.   But then, isn't there a special charm about all buds?   They hold the poetry of the future folded in their tiny sheaths, and a joy of expectancy that no fulfilment of opened flower can surpass. All the wonder of the springtime is hidden in the bud of a waiting flower; and when you come on millions of them at once—well, you just hold your breath and give yourself over to the marvel.

To the right of the track where the ridge slopes down to the distant harbour, the whitebeard buds spread in a thick carpet; in a few weeks it will be a fragrant white plot, but the woolly white sides are still hidden, and only the rosy

outsides are to be seen. Beyond the pink carpet the tall
spikes of the lysinema stand like sentinels amongst the bushes,
shedding a faint perfume abroad. Behind them again are the
banksias, their orange bottlebrushes shining amongst the dark
green leaves and making a fine feeding place for some New
Holland and white-cheeked honey-eaters. Already these birds
are busily building, and in a thick tangle of flowering needlebush and banksia I found the nest of the white-cheeked with
two newly-hatched chicks. As there is hardly a month in the
year when I have not found the nest of either of these two
birds, they cannot be taken as an indication of spring, but in a
small bushy turpentine in a cleared space I found what is always
the first sign of the new season—a tomtit's nest. It was
almost ready for eggs, and the little birds were busily flying to
and fro with soft feathers for the lining. Their sweet little
song trickled out on the clear air as they flew, and their happi-
ness and satisfaction were almost pathetic; for from the top
of a gum-tree not far away came the wail of their arch-enemy,
the bronze cuckoo, waiting to put her egg in the new nest, as
she does every year. But the tomtits did not seem to recognise
the melancholy note, and went cheerfully on with their work.
While I stood watching the gradual furnishing of the new home,
I found that the cuckoo was not the only foe the tomtits had.
All around I heard the courting note of the blackcaps, a low
soft whistle, quite distinct from their usual harsh "cheep
cheep;" and though I knew it would soon be time to look for

their tiny cradle-nests, I was rather astonished to see a pair
fly down from the top of the turpentine, pick a thread from the

Acacia longifolia

tomtit's bulky nest, and dart off with it to the topmost branch,
where already could be seen the foundation of their nest. Poor

little tomtits! they are so unsuspicious and good-natured, and it seems very unfair that their simplicity should be so imposed upon. Still, their nest is really rather ragged, and they could spare a few fibres for the blackcap's tiny home.

The only other birds I found building were the sweet-voiced, tawny-crowned honey-eaters, though everywhere I heard the courting notes, and saw birds evidently looking round for nesting spots.

But I had come out with an object in view. Last month I had found a lyre-bird's nest with an egg. Two weeks ago I visited it, and found the treasure still intact, and to-day I hoped to find the chick. So I left the tomtits to their building, and hurried on. At least I meant to hurry, but the path was one long series of interruptions. Such sweet interruptions they were, though, that I could not grumble. First there was a gorgeous clump of—oh, hateful name!—bossiaea, its flat stalks thickly covered with brown and golden pea blossoms that stood out in sharp contrast to the pale sandy soil. Then a little further on I found the first dillwynia of the year. Two or three plants were sparsely decorated with the opening yellow blossoms, but one small bush in a sheltered spot was covered with flowers, and stood out bravely as the forerunner of the golden army which will soon overrun the whole bush. Crimson spider-flowers were the next to hold my attention, and as I stopped to admire them I saw the clear yellow round flowers of the little hibbertia peering through a tangle of bushes. I pushed my way through the leaves, and found that the place was pink with the early boronia. I had not noticed it before, but now I found it at every step. It is not the prettiest of the boronias; its pink is perhaps rather crude, but very lovely it looked amongst the grey sand and dark green bushes. I stayed to pick an armful and a few stray spikes of tea-tree, which toned down the harshness. Then, as I left the shelter of the scribbly gums and the banksias, I came upon some more whitebeards, this time in full flower. They were a smaller kind than those I had passed before, not growing more than a foot high, but a brave little show the things made. I stopped to add a few sprays to my bunch, and also a piece of the beautiful red five-corner, and then I set my face to the track again, determined to loiter no longer. I had to stop once to pick some fine spikes of the pink sprengelia and a few pieces of the green five-corner, also some sprays of the honey-sweet native jasmine, whose white star flowers made a brilliant show, but after that I kept on my way. Perhaps the fact that my hands were as full as they would hold helped me in my determination, for it certainly requires great strength of mind to pass any of the first spring blossoms. But there was the nest at the end of my walk, and, I hoped, the little fluffy brown chick, so I hurried on.

I knew the way quite well, and less than half an hour's walk brought me to the spot. As I drew near I heard the voice of the lyre-bird down in the gully, and quickened my steps, hoping that, with luck, I might see the parent feeding the baby. I left my bunch of flowers in a shady spot, and scrambled over the rock to the big blue gum at whose foot was the nest. Ex-

Needlebush ~ *Hakea acicularis*

citedly I drew near, then stopped and listened. The ringing notes of the male bird floated up from the valley once again, but this time they were farther off, and there was no sign of the mother bird near. I would just peep in and have a look at the chick, then hide somewhere near, and wait for the parent to return. I stepped carefully forward, peeped in, and found— nothing. The nest was bare.

I am not a tearful subject, but you must admit that to have had my treasure robbed from under my very eyes was enough to make anyone weep with anger. I had been looking forward so much to seeing the baby bird, and had meant to bring my camera and photograph it. And now nothing remained but the empty nest. Some vandal had found my treasure trove, and I was left lamenting.

It was a very disappointed me that turned homewards. But already the sun was flinging crimson banners in the west, and the notes of the butcher-bird and the thickhead came full and sweet on the gentle breeze; high overhead swallows were skimming, and a flock of silvereyes went "peek-peeking" by. It wasn't a time to be sad. Despite the chill creeping up from the gullies, the joy of spring was in the air. Why should I cherish my disappointment about the loss of one treasure when the world holds so many?

> The faint fresh flame of the young year flushes
> From leaf to flower;

and the weeks to come will bring joys too many to grasp. So, clasping my sweet burden tighter in my arms, I marched towards the sunset, singing.

FLOWERS BLOOMING.

Hibbertia aspera
Tetratheca ericifolia
Zieria laevigata
Boronia ledifolia
Boronia poligalifolia
Correa reflexa   Native fuchsia
Ricinocarpus pinifolius   Native jasmine
Pimelea glauca
Dillwynia retorta
Bossiaea scolopendria   } Yellow pea-flowers
Acacia ulicifolia   Juniper-leafed wattle
Acacia brownii
Acacia myrtifolia   Myrtle-leafed wattle
Acacia suaveolens   Sweet-scented wattle
Acacia longifolia   Sydney golden wattle
Acacia terminalis   Port Jackson wattle
Cryptandra amara
Hakea sericea   Needlebush
Persoonia lanceolata
Banksia ericifolia
Banksia marginata   } Honeysuckles, or bottlebrushes
Olearia ramulosa   Snow bush
Styphelia longiflora
Styphelia tubiflora   } Five-corners
Astroloma humifusum
Astroloma pinifolium   } Ground berries
Leucopogon ericoides
Leucopogon virgatus   } Whitebeards
Epacris microphylla
Epacris longiflora   Native fuchsia
Epacris pulchella
Epacris purpurascens
Woollsia pungens   White heath
Monotoca elliptica   Pigeon berry

BIRDS BREEDING IN JULY.

Acanthiza chrysorrhoa	Tomtit or Yellow-rumped Thornbill
Phylidonyris novaehollandiae	New Holland Honeyeater
Phylidonyris nigra	White-cheeked Honeyeater
Melithreptus lunatus	Blackcap or White-naped Honeyeater
Zosterops lateralis	Silvereye
Pardalotus punctatus	Diamond-bird or Spotted Pardalote
Menura novaeseelandiae	Superb Lyrebird
Chrysococcyx lucidus plagosus	Golden Bronze Cuckoo

Lyrebird ~ Menura novaeseelandiae